Career Development, Assessment, and Counseling: Applications of the Donald E. Super C-DAC Approach

W. Larry Osborne
Steve Brown
Spencer Niles
Claire Usher Miner

CAREER DEVELOPMENT, ASSESSMENT, AND COUNSELING

10 9 8 7 6 5 4 3 2 1

American Counseling Association
5999 Stevenson Avenue
Alexandria, VA 22304

Director of Acquisitions
Carolyn Baker

Director of Publishing Systems
Michael Comlish

Cover by Cassidy Design

Library of Congress Cataloging-in-Publication Data

Career development, assessment, and counseling : the C-DAC approach of
   Donald E. Super / W. Larry Osborne . . . [et al.].
      p. cm.
   Includes bibliographical references and indexes.
   ISBN 1-55620-162-1 (alk. paper)
   1. Career development. 2. Vocational guidance. I. Osborne, W. Larry.
HF5381.C26528 1997
158.6—dc21

96-49704
CIP

Dedication

This book is dedicated, first of all, to Dr. Donald E. Super, who was a leader, colleague, mentor, and friend to the authors, and many others in the counseling profession.

It is also dedicated to our families, friends, and associates who have taught us about ourselves, others, living, and the process of career development.

Table of Contents

Preface

Career counseling is central to the counseling profession, and has been since the early 1900s. Donald E. Super spent more than 50 years of his professional life studying, researching, writing, and teaching about career development, and was internationally recognized as an authority in the field.

Dr. Super described some of his research and practical applications of it in one of his last professional articles, "Developmental Career Assessment and Counseling: The C-DAC Model" (*Journal of Counseling and Development*, 1992, 71, pp. 74–83, with Osborne, Walsh, Brown, and Niles).

The reviewer of the article (Fouad, 1992) stated that

> My main concern with the article is its brevity. The link between theory and practice is needed, and this article merely serves to whet the appetite. I wanted to know more about many aspects of the article—more about how the assessments fit together in a "real" case, more about how developmental counseling is implemented, and more about how developmental concerns affect the adult career client. (pp. 81–82)

This book is intended to meet that need, and was written at the suggestion of Donald Super and with his support. It provides an overview of some theory and research that gives rise to the Career Development, Assessment, and Counseling (C-DAC) model, a description of the test instruments that make up the assessment battery, and chapters on practical applications of the approach with high school students, university students, and adult clients.

We hope that the book will provide a clearer understanding of a valuable approach to career assessment and counseling, and further an even greater appreciation for the outstanding contributions of Dr. Donald E. Super to our understanding of the career development process.

Acknowledgments

The Career Development, Assessment, and Counseling (C-DAC) approach described in this book would not be possible without a half-century of research and effort by Donald E. Super, who died June 21, 1994 at age 83 in Savannah, Georgia.

Donald E. Super was born July 10, 1910 in Honolulu, Hawaii, and earned his Bachelor of Arts degree in 1932 and Master of Arts degree in 1936 from Oxford University in England. He was an assistant employment secretary at the Cleveland, Ohio, YMCA and an instructor in social sciences at Fenn College (now Cleveland State University) from 1932 to 1935, and director of the Cleveland Guidance Service and State Director of Guidance, National Youth Administration in Ohio from 1935 to 1936.

Donald Super married Anne-Margaret Baker of Savannah, Georgia, on September 12, 1936, and they had two sons: Robert, an architect-photographer in California, and Charles, a psychologist and professor at Pennsylvania State University. Mrs. Super died at home in Savannah on November 6, 1989 after an evening of talking and reading with her husband.

After his marriage, Donald Super was a graduate fellow and research assistant at Columbia University from 1936 to 1938, followed by an appointment as an assistant and associate professor at Clark University in Worcester, Massachusetts, from 1938 to 1942. During this period he earned his doctorate at Columbia University in 1940, then served as an aviation psychologist from 1942 to 1945, followed by an appointment as professor of psychology and education at Columbia University until his "first" retirement in 1975.

Dr. Super then went on to be a Visiting Fellow at Wolfson College and Senior Research Fellow at the National Institute for Careers Education and Counselling, Cambridge, England, from 1976 to 1979. He followed that with appointments as Honorary Fellow, National Institute for Careers Education and Counselling, Cambridge and Hatfield, England; International Coordinator for The Work Importance Study, Consultant in Counseling Psychology at the University of Georgia; Visiting Professor at the University of Florida; Consultant in Residence in the Department of Psychology at Armstrong State College in Savannah, Georgia; and Visiting Distinguished Professor in the Department of Counseling and Educational Development at the University of North Carolina at Greensboro.

Dr. Super had visiting and consulting appointments at many North American, South American, European, Asian, Australasian, and African universities, research and development institutes and organizations, government agencies, and corporations since 1949. He was awarded an Honorary Doctorate by the University of Lisbon in Portugal in 1983 and a Doctorate of Science by Oxford University in 1985, and held the rank of Professor Emeritus of Psychology and Education at Teachers College, Columbia University, at the time of his death.

Other honors acquired by Dr. Super include a Diplomate in Counseling Psychology from the American Board of Examiners in Psychology, a Fulbright Professor of Psychology at the University of Paris, Paris, France, from 1958 to 1959, the Distinguished Research Award from the American Counseling Association (1961), the Eminent Career Award given by the National Career Development Association in 1972, the Leona Tyler Award from the Division of Counseling Psychology of the American Psychological Association in 1981, and the Distinguished Contributions to the Applications of Psychology Award conferred by the American Psychological Association in 1983.

The contributions of Donald Super to the counseling profession are nearly too numerous to mention. He wrote more than 150 journal articles and books; coordinated the longitudinal Career Pattern Study, which studied the career development of over 100 men for more than 30 years; developed four psychological tests and inventories that contribute to the C-DAC model described in this book; was the founding president-elect from 1951 to 1953 of what is now known as the American Counseling Association; was one of four founding stockholders of the *Journal of Counseling Psychology*; served on the editorial boards of at least nine journals; was president of the Division of Counseling Psychology of the American Psychological Association from 1951 to 1952; had Fellow status in Clinical, Counseling, and Industrial and Organizational Psychology in the American Psychological Association; served as president of the National Career Development Association from 1969 to 1970; was a founding member of the American Psychological Society in 1988; and held appointed and elected positions in the International Association for Applied Psychology and the International Association for Educational and Vocational Guidance.

But no recounting of accomplishments, contributions, and awards can acknowledge the true measure of a person and what he meant to others. Donald E. Super was a man with presence, humor, energy, enthusiasm, devotion, creativity, and wisdom, who was an inspiration to many.

For all that he was, he shall always be remembered and treasured.

About the Authors

Larry Osborne is a member of the counselor education faculty at the University of North Carolina at Greensboro. He also is an Adjunct Program Associate at the Center for Creative Leadership, and has been an adjunct faculty member or visiting professor at seven universities. He has conducted training programs, workshops, and convention presentations throughout the United States and in England and Mexico. He also has held elected and appointed professional offices on the local, state, regional, and national levels, published widely in professional journals, co-authored books, and edited national publications. Dr. Osborne's current professional interests include career and leadership development counseling and group counseling, and he worked closely with Dr. Donald E. Super on a number of research projects over the last 8 years.

Steve Brown conducted research with Donald Super over a 5-year period, and made several presentations with him on the Career Development, Assessment, and Counseling (C-DAC) model at national and international conferences. He received his doctorate in Applied Behavioral Studies in Education with a specialization in Counseling Psychology from Oklahoma State University, and has been Director of the Counseling and Testing Center at the University of Georgia since 1987. While in this position, Dr. Brown has served on numerous university committees, been a member of several professional associations, held both elected and appointed offices in those associations and at the University of Georgia, and is a Licensed Professional Counselor in Georgia. His professional interests, other than career development, include organizational dynamics and structure, family systems, working with impaired professionals, and hypnosis.

Spencer Niles currently serves on the faculty for Counselor Education at the University of Virginia, where he teaches, among other things, master's and doctoral level courses in career counseling and career development. He also serves as the director of the Personal and Career Development Center, a counseling center sponsored by the University of Virginia to provide counseling services to adults in career transition. This counseling center serves as a research site for the application of the C-DAC model to adult career counseling clients. Dr. Niles has written numerous articles and delivered many presentations on the topics of career counseling and career development, serves on the editorial board for the *Career Development Quarterly*, is a member of the Ethics Committee and the Research

Committee for the National Career Development Association, and is President of the Virginia Career Development Association.

Claire Usher Miner resides in Austin, Texas. She has taught the C-DAC model in university career counseling and assessment courses, conducts local workshops on career change, has made convention presentations at the state, regional, and national levels, and has published 12 journal articles on a variety of topics within the career development field, such as training counselors using the C-DAC model, career counseling with student athletes, and postdegree supervision of counselors. She has served on the Editorial Board of the *Career Development Quarterly*, has been Secretary for the Association for Assessment in Counseling, and is an adjunct professor at St. Mary's University in San Antonio, Texas.

1

History and Background

The C-DAC (Career Development, Assessment, and Counseling) approach is a way of facilitating the career development of people across the life span. The approach is based on the career development theory and research of Dr. Donald E. Super, and assumes that certain aspects of one's career development can be assessed and influenced through test interpretation and career counseling.

The approach consists of administering at least five instruments that measure different dimensions of one's career development, and basing career counseling on their results.

These instruments include:

The Adult Career Concerns Inventory (ACCI) (Super, Thompson, Lindeman, Jordaan, & Myers, 1988a), which indicates to what stages of career development, and their corresponding coping skills, one is attending.

The Career Development Inventory (CDI) (Super et al., 1988b), a measure of attitudes and knowledge that are useful for facilitating stages of career development.

The Strong Interest Inventory (SII) (Strong, Campbell, & Hansen, 1985), which portrays interests that come from attitudes and knowledge related to stages of career development.

The Values Scale (VS) (Nevill & Super, 1989a), which gives information about values for which one would hope to find expression through vocational interests related to attitudes and knowledge and stages of career development.

The Salience Inventory (SI) (Nevill & Super, 1986a) is "the bottom line." It assesses the extent to which one participates in, is committed to, and expects to be involved with five major life roles in her or his career development, including working, studying, home and family, community service, and leisure activities. In effect, The Salience Inventory reflects how one's attention to career development stages, attitudes and knowledge about career development, vocational interests, and values all come together in a lifestyle.

WHY USE THE C-DAC APPROACH?

The C-DAC approach recognizes that, in an age of increasingly rapid cultural and economic change (McDaniels, 1989), no simple process of matching people and jobs can adequately meet the needs of individuals and society. It is built on the need to take into account the possibility and the likelihood of changes in individual needs, values, interests, and circumstances, and the changing nature of work, as people go through life. This approach cannot, of course, predict which changes in people or society will take place, or when these changes will occur, but it can take into account the probabilities as ascertained in test research, and in studies of occupations and of careers, and of the organization of work in industry and business (Arthur, Hall, & Lawrence, 1989; Bloom, 1964; McDaniels, 1989; Montross & Shinkman, 1992).

WHERE DID THE C-DAC APPROACH COME FROM?

The C-DAC approach, like most, has a varied ancestry spread out over many years, although its immediate parentage is the result of almost 50 years of research by Donald Super. Frank Parsons (1909) first wrote about matching people with jobs on the basis of concern for and work with youth making the transition from school to work. Donald Paterson, at the University of Minnesota, who provided the model made nationally and internationally useful by Beatrice Dvorak of the United States Department of Labor before, during, and after World War II, directed the pioneer scientific and technical work that established the matching process. From this work came a well-documented compendium, critique, and manual for the use of instruments for vocational assessment that became a standard resource in the training of vocational counselors. The method of matching people with certain characteristics to occupations was put into a simple, easily used, well-validated procedure by Holland in 1959 and was updated in 1985 (Holland, 1985).

The second set of ancestors also was spread out over more than one generation. The present career development model that gives rise to the C-DAC approach was foreshadowed by the life span study carried out in Austria by Buehler (1933), by a survey of adult men in California by Davidson and Anderson (1937), by another survey of adult men by Miller and Form (1951), and by texts and articles by Super (1942, 1957, 1983, 1990).

THE C-DAC APPROACH

Much of Super's research that has contributed to the C-DAC approach can be grouped into three categories, including a model of career development, maturity, or adaptability; a model of determinants related to career development; and a life career model.

Career development, maturity, or adaptability are three terms used for a set of related but complex factors, and are notions that underlie the ACCI. First, career *development* is an ongoing process, from birth to death, although we are not accustomed to thinking of declining and dying as development. Second, *maturity* is a state, usually thought of as the peak of development, with a career perhaps having no peak, one peak, or several peaks. Third, *adaptability* is the ability to cope with career developmental and adaptation tasks, while recognizing that the capacity to do so does not exist evenly throughout one's life and may, in fact, show many peaks and valleys. Therefore, as one moves through life, various stages of career development are experienced with differing tasks encountered, as is shown in Figure 1.1.

The ease with which one moves through these stages and successfully adapts to them is the result of many factors, as shown in Figure 1.2. This graphic representation of career determinants is a Norman church door with two bases, two fluted columns, two capitals that crown them integrating the left-hand column (the individual with her or his traits) with the right-hand column (society and its institutions with their characteristics), and the superimposed arch that depicts the major life career stages, role self-concepts, and self or person who is the keystone, the decision maker. The self is depicted as the keystone because no matter what the internal and external pressures, it is, in the last analysis, the individual who makes the decision about how to handle one or another of these pressures, whether they are personal, familial, social, political, or economic.

As one moves through these stages and contends with the various career determinants, she or he plays various life roles that are the basis for the SI. The Life Career Rainbow (Super, 1990; Super in Montross & Shinkman, 1992) (see Figure 1.3) portrays the development or unfolding of the life career of a person from birth until death.

The two outside arcs of the rainbow show the name of the life stage and the approximate ages of transition from one stage to another. The other arcs represent the various roles that one plays throughout life during these stages and at particular ages, including child, pupil–student, leisurite, citizen, worker, spouse, homemaker, parent, and pensioner or annuitant following later.

It cannot be overemphasized that these ages are not precise endings and beginnings of stages; they are ages at which these transitions are

FIGURE 1.1 Life Stages and Substages

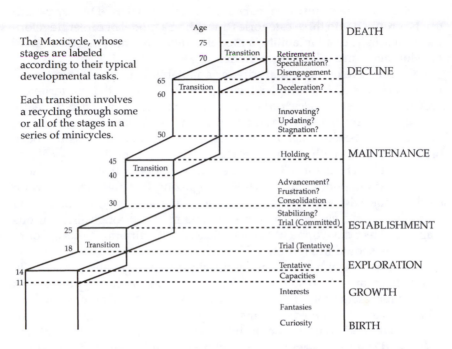

The Maxicycle, whose stages are labeled according to their typical developmental tasks.

Each transition involves a recycling through some or all of the stages in a series of minicycles.

Source: *Career Choice and Development: Applying Contemporary Theories to Practice, Second Edition*, by D. E. Super, edited by D. Brown. San Francisco: Jossey-Bass, 1990.

often noted, but for some they come earlier and for others later. Many also cycle through several stages as they make transitions, change jobs or occupations, become disabled, and leave or reenter the labor market and the labor force. Thus, these two rainbows could have breaks in the worker roles at times of educational or job transition, and in some versions, when the Life Career Rainbow is used to portray the involvement and commitment of an individual to various roles, darker or lighter shading or coloring may be used to depict greater or lesser commitment to a role.

The width of the shading of an arc can also be used to depict the time devoted to participation in a role, and the depth (darkness or lightness) of the shading may show the amount of affect invested in the role and the commitment to it. No distinction is made in this model among position, job, occupation, company, or career in the sense of an idealized sequence of increasingly self-fulfilling jobs and occupations.

Thus, the rainbow depicts the person's career in terms of a life span and life space, formed by nine major roles played first only as a child with the other roles occurring later during five life stages.

FIGURE 1.2   A Segmental Model of Career Development

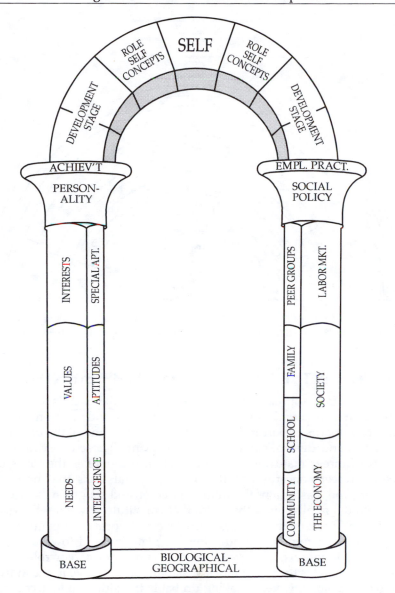

SOURCE: *Career Choice and Development: Applying Contemporary Theories to Practice, Second Edition*, by D. E. Super, edited by D. Brown. San Francisco: Jossey-Bass, 1990.

FIGURE 1.3 The Life-Career Rainbow

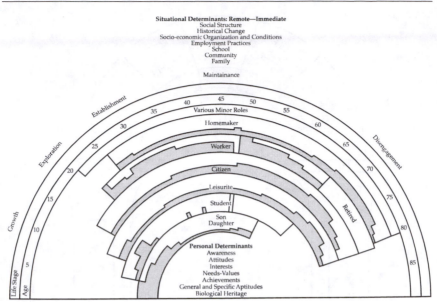

Source: *Career Choice and Development: Applying Contemporary Theories to Practice, Second Edition,* by D. E. Super, edited by D. Brown. San Francisco: Jossey-Bass, 1990.

HOW IS THE C-DAC APPROACH IMPLEMENTED?

The C-DAC approach involves determining the client's knowledge of the stages of occupational careers, of the structure and functioning of the world of work (its opportunities and requirements), and of the principles, processes, and data of career decision making. These constitute vital aspects of career maturity. This approach also identifies the focus of a person's career concerns and the developmental tasks that he or she confronts, and it ascertains the values placed on and sought in the occupational, study, family, and other roles that constitute a career—the essentials for self-fulfillment. It assesses the levels of vocational maturity in a second way, examining attitudes toward planning and toward inquiry into educational, occupational, familial, and other career roles. And, finally, it estimates the possibilities of stability and change in the individual over the next few years, taking probable transitions into account.

Developmental career counseling using the C-DAC approach initially involves sharing with the individual or group an understanding of the normal sequence and nature of life stages and of life space. The Life Career Rainbow (see Figure 1.3) is a good teaching device for this purpose (Super, 1990).

The ACCI profile can then be discussed either in group counseling or individually in counseling interviews to help the client understand her or his position in the life cycle and the career development tasks that are likely to be encountered.

This can be followed by the CDI to consider the attitudes and knowledge of the client that can be applied to these tasks, and her or his interests according to the SII. After this, what the individual seeks while pursuing a career, now and in the future, can be considered with the SI's emphasis on life roles and the VS's focus on what the individual seeks to attain in life in those roles. The tendency for roles and values to change somewhat with increasing age can be considered to broaden perspectives and to extend horizons.

Finally, these developmental data can be applied to the results of other interest inventories, aptitude batteries, and discussions of educational, occupational, and familial objectives, leading to the formulation of long-term plans and of strategies for immediate action to facilitate their attainment. Possible changes in interests, values, and careers, together with economic and industrial changes, also are essential to consider in long-range planning.

The order in which a battery such as this should be given is considered in each of the current C-DAC research locations, including the University of North Carolina at Greensboro, the University of Virginia, the University of Georgia, and Austin, Texas. Three basic sequences have emerged, each of which has much to commend it. After general orientation to the purpose and nature of the battery, they are as follows:

Sequence A. (1) CDI/ACCI, (2) SII, (3) VS, (4) SI
Sequence B. (1) SII, (2) VS, (3) CDI/ACCI, (4) SI
Sequence C. This sequence is based on the objectives of the assessment and the needs of the client, with the possibility of adding other tests or making substitutions based on the same considerations. Some current additions or substitutions include the Myers-Briggs Type Indicator at the University of North Carolina at Greensboro, and the Osipow and Spokane Occupational Stress Inventory at the University of Virginia. Others that have been added at various times are Osipow's Career Development Scale and Krumboltz's Career Beliefs Inventory.

The logic is as follows: Sequence A begins with looking at the developmental stage, the tasks, or concerns the individual faces, and whether he or she is a student (CDI) or adult (ACCI). These are questions that may have been considered in the intake interview or that the counselor-assessor believes are best addressed before considering aptitudes, interests, values, and life roles. With an understanding of the readiness of the student to make career decisions, or of the concerns the adult feels for the various tasks of exploration, establishment, maintenance, and decline, the process moves on to examine the counselee's interests, the values that underlie them, and the relative importance of the major life roles in which these values and interests might find outlets.

Sequence B, on the other hand, begins with the client's interests, because some people come to counseling seeking to find or to confirm an occupational choice; they ask about what major or what occupation they should choose. Here the counselor shows a readiness to begin where the client wants to begin; meeting this need, it is then possible to ask whether the interest inventory scores may be taken as indexes of wise choices or should be viewed as signs of what might be good fields of activity to explore and to try out before making a choice. This can be followed by a consideration of the values one holds and how they may find expression through these interests, the skills the client may have for addressing career development tasks, and how all of this plays out in one's life roles. Many less mature students, women reentering the work force, and displaced men need this approach.

Sequence C, as stated earlier, provides flexibility and the opportunity to collect data of theoretical or practical interest (e.g., in the case of the CDI, insights into readiness to make career decisions and obstacles in the way of making them). It is a sequence that also allows for the counselor to "pick and choose" instruments and an order of administration that fits the "flow" of the career counseling process with a particular client.

The novel tests (ACCI/CDI and the SI) give counselors and personnel workers an objective means of assessing the need to explore widely or to explore in depth, and the readiness to make a choice of major field in school or college or of an occupation in entering or making a change in the labor market. In leisure counseling the focus may be on Sequence B, because the goal here may be to generally explore one's lifestyle and how to order it in a comfortable manner, rather than make a specific decision about a particular occupation.

The C-DAC battery contains no aptitude tests; this is because in many educational and some corporate situations such data are already available for admissions, selection, or appraisal programs, and no additional aptitude testing is needed. When this is not the case, batteries such as the Differential Aptitude Test, the Armed Services Vocational Aptitude Battery, and the Miller Analogies Test (university and adult) might be considered (Anastasi, 1988).

Whether all of the testing is done in one session, several sessions, or on a take-home basis can vary with the situation, reasons for doing the assessment, and the chosen sequence of test administration. In any case, the length of the assessment process needs to be explained and accepted, the benefits from the depth with which it probes and the scope it covers made clear, and a program arranged accordingly (Super et al., 1992).

SUMMARY

The C-DAC approach has a history dating back to the early part of this century, with a developmental, life span basis largely derived from the work of Donald E. Super and incorporating the use of five instruments (the Adult Career Concerns Inventory, the Career Development Inventory, the Strong Interest Inventory, The Values Scale, and The Salience Inventory) to provide information for the client's career decision making.

The following chapters include a more detailed discussion of the C-DAC test instruments and presentations on how to use them with high school students, university students, and adults.

2

Discussion of C-DAC Instruments

Tests have provided important information to facilitate the career development process during much of the twentieth century. This chapter deals with the use of tests in career development, the various test instruments that make up the Career Development, Assessment, and Counseling (C-DAC) battery, and case studies to demonstrate how the battery can be used in career counseling.

THE USES OF TESTS IN CAREER INTERVENTIONS

One of the most common statements made by career counseling clients is that they want to "take a test that will tell them what they should do." For many clients and counselors an inextricable link exists between the terms "career development" and "assessment." This link results from a long history of using tests to aid in the acquisition of self-information for the purpose of matching individuals to jobs. Since the early 1900s up to the present day, testing has been an important ingredient in most career intervention models. The link between career development and assessment, however, has been controversial. For example, E.G. Williamson and Carl Rogers disagreed over the use of aptitude assessment in career counseling. Others have argued that the link between career counseling and testing should be severed as a result of factors such as the low predictive validity of tests, bias in test development and interpretation, and the fostering of client dependency on the counselor due to the overreliance on tests in career counseling (Crites, 1969; Goldman, 1971; Healy, 1990; Weinrach, 1979).

In response to some of these criticisms, Prediger (1974) suggested that, whenever possible, counselors should use comprehensive assessment programs that include self-administered and self-interpreted assessments. As a general guideline, practitioners should use assessment results as just one source of information in career counseling. In most cases test information is best used as a stimulus for further career and self-exploration. Avoiding the use of psychometric jargon, clearly explaining the purposes and limitations of assessment instruments, and actively soliciting client participation in the test interpretation process will enable career counselors to maximize the usefulness of test information in career counseling.

The uses of career assessment instruments have been discussed and classified in various ways (cf. Herr & Cramer, 1992; Isaacson & Brown, 1993; Spokane, 1991; Zunker, 1990). Regardless of the classification system used, it is clear that the purposes for using tests in career counseling have increased dramatically in the 1900s. In the first half of the twentieth century, testing in career assessment was primarily for the purpose of matching clients to occupational and educational options. Today assessment devices are used in career counseling to measure factors such as aptitudes, interests, values, personality types, decisional status, beliefs about career development, and level of career development. In this regard Super (1983) noted that the traditional model of matching people to jobs "in order to predict and to ensure them success and satisfaction" (p. 555) is not sufficient.

Specifically, the matching model of career assessment does not address some important factors in career development. For example, the client's readiness for career decision making (i.e., career maturity) is not considered in the matching model. Yet, there is "good objective evidence as to the existence of great individual differences in career maturity" (Super, 1983, p. 557). Adults who lack the necessary information, or have not engaged in the required planning as students, are "not sufficiently mature to have mature and stable traits" (Super, 1983, p. 557). For many students occupational futures seem too distant for them to benefit from the review of aptitude and interest test results. In such instances, the focus must be on increasing the student's readiness for career decision making prior to proceeding to aptitude, interest, and values testing.

Counselors using the traditional matching model of assessment also fail to consider individual differences in life-role importance. Yet research in the area of "work alienation and job involvement has made it clear that not everyone is work motivated" (Super, 1983, p. 558). Everyone does not participate at equal levels with equal levels of commitment in the major roles of life (e.g., worker, student, citizen, leisurite, homemaker). By examining the role salience of clients, the Developmental Assessment Model proposed by Super (1983) accounts for the issues of career maturity, life-role importance, and "the search for a good match of developing interests, values, and aptitudes with those characterizing a field of work and other life career roles" (p. 562).

THE DEVELOPMENTAL ASSESSMENT MODEL

The Developmental Assessment Model consists of four steps: (1) preview, (2) depth-view, (3) assessment of all data, and (4) counseling. The preview step involves conducting an intake interview and preliminary assessment of the client's concerns and situation. In the second step, the counselor and client explore the relative importance the client places on major life roles (e.g., student, worker, citizen, leisurite, and homemaker). It is also important to explore the values the client seeks to express in each life role. The second part of the depth-view involves determining the client's readiness for career decision making or career maturity. Of primary concern is the degree to which the client exhibits planfulness, exploratory attitudes, decision-making skills, the possession of world-of-work information, and realism in self and situational assessment. Lastly, the depth-view focuses on ability and interest assessment. Step 3 in the model involves the review of all data with the goal of considering matches between the client and occupations as well as nonoccupational roles. The final step in the model is counseling. Counseling involves the collaborative review and discussion of assessment data. The assessment results are revised or accepted by the client and planning for next steps is done. A goal at this point is to help clients to

> see themselves as individuals coping with certain developmental tasks, at a stage in life at which they are expected, and to some degree may expect themselves, to make certain decisions and acquire certain competencies and statuses. (Super, 1983, p. 559)

THE USES OF THE C-DAC BATTERY IN DEVELOPMENTAL ASSESSMENT

The implementation of the Developmental Assessment Model can be accomplished through the use of the C-DAC battery. For example, for helping clients understand their degree of commitment to work and other life roles, the counselor can administer The Salience Inventory (SI). Counselors can use the Career Development Inventory (CDI) to determine if clients possess readiness for career decision making. To assess planfulness (a principal dimension of career maturity), and help clients become aware of career developmental tasks, the Adult Career Concerns Inventory (ACCI) can be used. To examine if a client's interests and values match with various educational and occupational options, the Strong Interest Inventory (SII) and The Values Scale (VS) can be used. These are just brief examples of the information the C-DAC battery can provide. With the

13

use of the instruments comprising the C-DAC battery, the Developmental Assessment Model

> identifies the focus of a person's career concerns and the developmental tasks that he or she confronts. It ascertains the values placed on and sought in the occupational, study, family, and other roles that constitute a career—the essential for self-fulfillment. It assesses the level of vocational maturity . . . examining attitudes toward planning and toward inquiry into educational, occupational, familial, and other career roles. It estimates the possibilities of stability and change in the individual over the next few years, taking probable transitions into account. (Super et al., 1992, p. 75)

The C-DAC battery is being used in secondary schools, higher education, private career counseling, and corporate environments. It is appropriate for fostering development, increasing awareness of developmental tasks, lifestyle planning, career revitalization, and making occupational or educational choices. In order to examine the usefulness of the assessment instruments within the C-DAC battery, discussion now focuses on the individual instruments and their separate and combined contributions to career counseling.

ADULT CAREER CONCERNS INVENTORY

The ACCI, which was first developed in order to collect data in the final follow-up of the Career Pattern Study (Zelkowitz, 1974), is based on Super's model of career adaptability in adulthood (Super, 1977, 1985). More specifically, Super contends that five factors are important in examining career adaptability for adults. These factors are (1) planfulness or time perspective, (2) exploration, (3) information, (4) decision making, and (5) reality orientation.

Although career adaptability is a multidimensional quality, several studies have found planfulness to be the most important group factor related to career maturity (Gribbons & Lohnes, 1968; Myers, Lindeman, Forrest, & Super, 1971). The term *planfulness* in this instance relates to the tendency to plan ahead based on a sense of control, an awareness of the past and anticipation of the future, and a sense of self-esteem. The ACCI is a 61-item inventory that was designed to assess planfulness in young and in mature adults.

In assessing planfulness, the ACCI measures the degree of concern expressed for the major developmental tasks of an adult occupational career. Total scores are provided for the career developmental stages of exploration, establishment, maintenance, and disengagement and for the developmental tasks within each stage (e.g., crystallization, specification, implementation).

Reliability and Validity

A study conducted by Halpin, Ralph, and Halpin (1990) reported alpha coefficients (the means of all split-half coefficients from different splittings of a test) of .95, .95, .94, .93, and .94 for the ACCI scales measuring exploration, establishment, maintenance, disengagement, and career change, respectively. Additional reliability estimates (median = .90) have been reported for two groups: 68 academic professionals and 331 corporate employees (Super et al., 1988a). Data provided in a dissertation study conducted by Mahoney (1986) revealed alpha coefficients at .90 for the ACCI.

Studies by Mahoney (1986), Morrison (1977), and Stout, Slocum, and Cron (1987), provide evidence for the construct, concurrent, and predictive validity of the ACCI. Using subjects from the Career Pattern Study, Zelkowitz (1974) found that men who were administered the ACCI at the midcareer stage were more concerned with the tasks of the Establishment and Maintenance stages than with those of the Exploration and Disengagement stages. A study by Cron and Slocum (1986) found support for the criterion-related validity of the ACCI. Cron and Slocum found the ACCI to be a useful measure in distinguishing between the job attitudes and the career stages of a sample of salespeople (e.g., salespeople in the Exploration stage of a sample of salespeople; they were less involved in their jobs, did not feel that their job was challenging, and did not feel as successful as salespeople in other career stages). Halpin et al. (1990) also concluded that the ACCI was a valid measure of career concerns for the sample of graduate nursing students in their study.

Administration and Scoring

The ACCI is self-administered, self-scorable, and can be machine or template scored. It takes from 15 to 30 minutes to complete and total administration time is 20 to 40 minutes. Percentile norms for men and women are provided in the manual by age brackets as follows: under 25, 25 to 34, 35 to 44, and 45 and older. Percentiles are useful in making comparisons with one's age and sex group. Total scores are provided for the developmental stages of Exploration (EX), Establishment (ES), Maintenance (MA), and Disengagement (DI) as well as for the developmental tasks within each stage (e.g., crystallization, specification, implementation). Each stage score is composed of 15 items measuring respondents' current levels of concern on a 5-point Likert scale with a rating of 1 being equal to "no concern" and 5 indicating "great concern." The ratings given to the items within the respective stages are summed and then averaged.

In each of the four stages, three career developmental tasks are measured by five item scales. The scoring procedure is the same for tasks and stages. Item 61 is a measure of the client's career change status and response options from a score of 1 ("I am not considering making a career change") to a score of 5 ("I have recently made a change and am settling down in the new field").

The Case of Jenny

Jenny is a 35-year-old female who came to the counseling center for help in making a career decision. She was recently divorced and had been working as a full-time homemaker for the past 12 years. She had two daughters ages 12 and 8. Prior to this, Jenny worked as a nurse (RN) in her local hospital. Her main concerns seemed to be related to whether she should consider other occupational options, return to nursing, or return to college. She stated that she did not really enjoy work as a nurse and she was less than enthusiastic about returning to her previous occupation.

The results of the ACCI (see Figure 2.1) indicated that her concerns were clearly focused on Exploration. She was especially concerned with the career developmental tasks of crystallizing and specifying. In other words, Jenny was interested in finding out about jobs that would be appropriate for her interests, skills, and values. She was not concerned with establishing herself in an occupation or with looking forward to life in retirement.

As these results were reviewed with her, Jenny became clearer as to the focus of her career decision making. Jenny's low scores related to the tasks of establishment and maintenance helped her to clarify that she did not want to return to nursing. When asked whether she had considered updating her nursing skills and applying them in more innovative nursing-related career options, Jenny stated that the thought of pursuing additional training in nursing was "depressing" to her. In this regard, Jenny's relatively secure financial situation helped to make this a more viable option for her. After discussing the ACCI results, Jenny stated that she was eager to explore the relationship between occupational options and her interests, skills, and values.

CAREER DEVELOPMENT INVENTORY

Super's Career Pattern study stimulated interest in the construct of "career maturity," or the readiness of youth to make occupational decisions. This longitudinal study of 123 ninth-grade males was the forerunner of John Crites's (1978) first measure of career maturity, the Career Maturity

FIGURE 2.1 Individual Analysis of Career Concerns

Individual Analysis of Career Concerns

Name **Jenny**   Age **35**

Compared with **35 - 44 Women**   Date **9/94**

Consulting Psychologists Press, Inc.
Palo Alto, CA 94303

The ACCI can be self-scored to yield a profile based on the clusters of career development tasks of most concern to you. The procedures for self-scoring and profile analysis are:

1. On the Career Concerns Chart below, enter the distribution of ratings for each of the groups of 5 items in each substage. For example, if for items 1 to 5, you marked 1 for two items, 2 for two items, and 3 for one item, you would enter those numbers in the appropriate spaces on the Crystallization line.

2. Then compute the average score for the substage by dividing the weighted sum by the number of items in the group. For the above example, the weighted sum would be 2+4+3=9, divided by 5 equals 1.8. Enter the weighted sum and average in the appropriate columns. Follow the same procedure for each substage and stage.

3. Circle the number of the response you chose for Item 61.

4. Plot your Career Stage and Substage Profile below by marking with a capital X on the appropriate line the location of each of the four Stage averages, and with a small x each of the Substage averages. Connect the small x's in each Stage to draw the four profiles of your current career concerns. Intraindividual interpretations of average Substage scores are usually more insight-producing than are Stage scores because of present and future orientations and recycling.

5. Convert the raw scores (5-point ratings) into percentiles with the appropriate table in the Manual or from local norms. Percentiles make it possible to compare one person with a group of relevant people, and average ratings on the 5-point scale help when a person compares him or herself using the profile.

6. Record for each Substage the number of items rated either 4 or 5 to show the clustering of major concerns and to help interpret Stage and Substage averages in the Career Concerns Chart below.

CAREER CONCERNS CHART

Items	Career Concerns	None 1	Little 2	Some 3	Cons. 4	Great 5	Weighted Sum	Average
A: EXPLORATION STAGE								
1–5	Crystallization			1	1	3	22	4.4
6–10	Specification				1	4	24	4.8
11–15	Implementation		2	1	2		15	3
1–15	TOTAL EXPLORATION						61	4.1
B: ESTABLISHMENT STAGE								
16–20	Stabilizing	2	1	2			10	2
21–25	Consolidating	3	1	1			8	1.6
26–30	Advancing	2	1	2			10	2
16–30	TOTAL ESTABLISHMENT						28	1.9
C: MAINTENANCE STAGE								
31–35	Holding	4	1				7	1.4
36–40	Updating	5					5	1
41–45	Innovating	4	1				6	1.2
31–45	TOTAL MAINTENANCE						18	1.2
D: DISENGAGEMENT STAGE								
46–50	Deceleration	4	1				7	1.4
51–55	Retirement Planning	2	2	1			9	1.8
56–60	Retirement Living	4	1				6	1.2
46–60	TOTAL DISENGAGEMENT						22	1.5
61	CAREER CHANGE STATUS	1	2	③	4	5 (Circle Response)		

CAREER STAGE AND SUBSTAGE PROFILE

Substages	Amount of Current Concern (None 1.0 – Little 2.0 – Some 3.0 – Cons. 4.0 – Great 5.0)	%-ile	Number of Concerns Rated 4 (Considerable) or 5 (Great)
Crystallization	x		4
Specification	x		5
Implementation	X	9th	2
			11
Stabilizing	x		—
Consolidating	x		—
Advancing	X	17th	—
			—
Holding	x		—
Updating	x		—
Innovating	X	1st	—
			—
Deceleration	x		—
Retirement Planning	x		—
Retirement Living	X	9th	—
			—

Inventory, which has since been criticized for its lack of validity and withdrawn from publication.

According to Super, career maturity is a complex, multidimensional construct that has both attitudinal and cognitive elements. The attitudinal elements measured by the CDI are (a) planfulness about one's career development (CP scale), and (b) the willingness to engage in exploratory activities related to the developmental tasks of exploration and establishment (CE scale). The cognitive elements are (a) knowledge of career decision-making principles (DM scale), (b) knowledge of what it takes to get a job and succeed at it (WW scale), and (c) knowledge of a career field in which one is currently interested (PO scale).

Administration and Scoring

The CDI is produced in two forms: the High School Form appropriate for grades 8 to 12, and the College/University Form appropriate for traditional-aged undergraduate and graduate students. Both forms are identical in format but the items differ in content. The items reflect appropriate planning and exploratory attitudes and activities, as well as knowledge of occupations, for these two populations. Part II of the instrument, which yields a score on the PO scale, should not be administered to students below the 11th grade, because the ability to answer these questions comes only with maturity (Super, Thompson, Lindeman, Jordaan, & Myers, 1988c, p. 1).

The CDI may be administered to individuals or to groups and consists of a total of 120 items. Part I, which includes the items loading on the CP, CE, DM, and WW scales, contains 80 multiple-choice items and takes approximately 40 minutes to complete. Part II, which includes the multiple-choice items used to score the PO scale, contains 40 items and takes about 20 minutes to complete. The instrument is computer scored, and standard scores are derived based on national norms from the subject's grade-level and gender group. National percentile scores are also produced. These scores are yielded on the two attitudinal scales (CP and CE), the three cognitive scales (DM, WW, and PO), and three combined scales (CDA, CDK, and COT). CDA, the combined attitudinal score, is a combination of the CP and CE scales; CDK, the combined cognitive score, is a combination of the DM and WW scales; and COT, which combines the CP, CE, DM, and WW scales, is a reasonable estimate of overall career maturity.

Reliability and Validity

Cronbach alpha coefficients for the School Form, calculated for both genders within grade groups, show a median reliability of .86 for the combined scales, .89 for the CP scale, .78 for the CE scale, and .84 for the WW scale. The DM and PO scales have median alphas of .67 and .60, respectively (Super et al., 1988c, p. 14), and therefore should be used with caution in making individual judgments based on these scale scores.

To establish test–retest reliability, 668 high school students in two schools (one suburban, the other rural) completed a 3-week time interval study. For the students in the rural school, the correlations ranged from .61 for the PO scale to .84 for the COT scale. For the students in the suburban school, the correlations ranged from .63 for the PO scale to .82 for the COT scale. Only the PO, DM, and WW scales have reliabilities below .70, "although still indicative of satisfactory stability over a three-week interval" (Super et al., 1988c, p. 18).

For the College and University Form, 111 freshmen at a large state university completed a test–retest study with a 2-week interval. Correlations for the CDI scales ranged from .43 for the WW scale to .89 for the CP scale. The DM, WW, PO, and CDK correlations fell below .70, indicating that these scales should be used with caution for individual decision-making purposes.

Construct validity of the CDI has been established through correlational studies, factor analyses, and discriminant analyses. For example, the CDI Manual reports that (a) scores on all the scales increase from the 9th grade to the 12th grade, although the 11th grade means for DM, WW, PO, and CDK are slightly higher than the 12th grade means; (b) gender differences are only found for the cognitive scales, with females tending to score higher (consistent with their higher academic achievement, which has been found to correlate with the cognitive scales); (c) the attitude scales are not correlated significantly with scholastic ability; (d) students in honors classes scored higher on the cognitive scales; (e) in the higher grades, students in college preparatory and business programs scored higher on the cognitive scales than those in general or vocational programs; (f) students in vocational programs scored higher on the attitudinal scales, perhaps reflecting more immediate concern for vocational decision making (Super et al., 1988c, p. 17); and (g) two dimensions of career maturity, attitudinal and cognitive, have been found through factor analyses.

In addition, Luzzo (1993) found that the DM scale of the CDI was highly correlated with an interview method of assessing decision-making skill among undergraduate students and satisfied all the requirements of Campbell and Fiske's (1959) multitrait, multimethod procedure for establishing construct validity. Dykeman (1983) also found that the DM scale was significantly correlated with a measure of work effectiveness among a sample of drop-out-prone ninth graders. Seifert (1991) found significant correlations between the CP scale and vocational choice criteria for samples of Austrian high school students.

One predictive validity study (Dupont, 1992) was located on a French version of the CDI in use in Quebec schools. Three hundred sixty-five seniors in two secondary schools, who were administered the CDI, were tracked for 1 year afterward. The means of the students who persevered in their initial occupational choices were significantly higher than the nonpersevering students for the CP, DM, and WW scales. However, those students who were satisfied with their occupational choices scored higher than the dissatisfied students on only one CDI scale, Career Planning. Siefert (1991) also found that the CP score for Austrian 11th graders was a significant predictor of vocational choice criteria (such as information about career options, length of time considering the preferred choice, reduced career choice concerns, and appropriateness of preferences) among 12th graders. Overall, studies of the CDI's reliability and validity continue to support its psychometric soundness (Johnson, 1985, p. 140).

The Case of Jeffrey

Jeffrey is a ninth grader who was recently administered a battery of career assessments, including the CDI. He is hoping to attend a 4-year college or university and lists "engineer" as his occupational choice. Jeffrey is currently involved in extracurricular activities, football and basketball. He also is working in landscaping and has been employed in the past as a scoreboard keeper.

Jeffrey's attitudinal scores on the CDI indicate that he has not yet given much thought or planning to his future career (44th percentile on CP), but he shows much willingness to engage in exploratory activities (96th percentile on CE) (see Table 2.1).

Overall, he has positive attitudes about career planning and exploration, and he is likely to be a willing partner with the counselor in the exploration process (81st percentile on CDA).

TABLE 2.1   Career Development Inventory

CDI Scale	Percentile Scores
Career Planning (CP)	44
Career Exploration (CE)	96
Decision Making (DM)	74
World-of-Work Information (WW)	51
Preferred Occupation (PO)	Not Applicable
Career Development Attitudes (CDA)	81
Career Development Knowledge (CDK)	67
Career Orientation Total (COT)	70

Jeffrey's cognitive scores on the CDI indicate some areas for development. His knowledge of career decision-making principles is above average (74th percentile on DM), but his knowledge of what it takes to find a job and succeed at one is only average as compared with other ninth-grade males (51st percentile on WW). These scores indicate a need for Jeffrey to acquire more broad-based information about the world of work in general before specifying a career direction. Jeffrey should be encouraged to engage in more exploration before narrowing down his choice to any particular field. Career guidance and education activities should facilitate Jeffrey's wide-ranging exploration of the world of work.

THE STRONG INTEREST INVENTORY

The new 1994 revision of the SII represents over 65 years of development, and is based on data collected on more than 55,000 people in 50 different occupations during 1992 and 1993. This sample is more ethnically diverse than any previous sample with representation from all socioeconomic and educational backgrounds. The intent of this revision was to update the SII by developing new Occupational Scales to represent "emerging and growth" occupations. Data were collected from current occupational groups to update the basis of those Occupational Scales already in existence. The research form of the new SII contained all 325 items of the previous instrument, and 54 new items intended to be more current. These items measured the same content areas as items on the previous version of the SII, and addressed new content areas that contributed to other scales on the instrument. The 1994 edition of the SII includes 317 items: 282 taken from the previous edition in their original or slightly modified form, and 35 new items more reflective of our current society.

Development of the Strong Interest Inventory

The Strong Vocational Interest Blank (SVIB), the predecessor of the SII, was developed by E. K. Strong, Jr. in 1927. The SVIB scores represented the degree of similarity between an individual's interests and those of other individuals who were employed in various occupations. Although Strong attempted to group occupations into scales that had similar characteristics, he had difficulty developing scales that had strong psychometric qualities. As a result, other researchers (Campbell, Borgen, Eastes, Johannsson, & Peterson, 1968) turned their attention to developing what is now called the Basic Interest Scales. The psychometric qualities of the Basic Interest Scales were acceptable, but they did not provide a framework for the establishment of a functional organization of interests and their relationship to occupations.

21

General Occupational Themes

It was John Holland (1959) who first proposed the use of six categories of occupations that could be applied to the occupations included in the SVIB. Campbell and Hansen (1972) and Hansen and Johansson (1972) developed scales of SVIB items for Holland's six categories that are the basis of the Occupational Theme Scales and the subsequent profile scores of the SII. Thus the SII Occupational Theme Scales are the same as Holland's six work environments: Realistic, Investigative, Artistic, Social, Enterprising, and Conventional.

Realistic occupations are those related to more physically challenging jobs, those that require strength and good motor coordination, and generally are low in social interaction. Examples include military occupations, police officer, engineer, and forester.

Investigative occupations are those related to science, mathematics, and medical alternatives; they usually are task oriented, asocial, and require higher than average intellectual abilities. Occupations relevant to this theme would include biologist, psychologist, and veterinarian.

The Artistic Occupational Theme is represented by occupations that are less structured, provide opportunity for creative endeavors, and allow individual expression. The occupations in this theme also are somewhat introspective and asocial. Examples of occupations related to the Artistic Theme include musician, broadcaster, fine artist, and librarian.

The Social Occupational Theme provides opportunities for those who are more humanistic and sociable, individuals who like to work in groups with good interpersonal skills. Some occupational options for those preferring the Social Theme are minister, social worker, and elementary teacher.

The Enterprising Theme is for those who are driven to succeed economically, individuals who tend to dominate and lead with a desire for power and status. Occupations compatible with Enterprising interests include marketing executive, investments manager, and restaurant manager.

The Conventional Occupational Theme is similar to the Enterprising Occupational Theme, but is less social. People in this category like structure, material possessions, and status. Conventional occupations include accountant, secretary, and dietician.

More detail on the General Occupational Theme Scales can be obtained from the *Manual of the SVIB-SCII* (Hansen & Campbell, 1985). Additional information on Holland's work environments, the basis of the General Occupational Theme Scales, can be found in *Making vocational choices: A theory of careers* (Holland, 1973).

The General Occupational Themes for the 1994 SII have the same names and relationships to Holland's six areas as previous editions. Some of the items have been changed to enhance reliability, and some of the scales include more items. The item content is the same as scales on previous editions of the SII to maintain content and construct validity. Hence, interpretation of the scales virtually remains unchanged.

Basic Interest Scales

The Basic Interest Scales follow the General Occupational Theme Scales on the SII. The Basic Interest Scales were developed to be more statistically pure, whereas the General Occupational Theme Scales represent a conceptual organization that more closely reflects the smaller number of dimensions that are considered to underlie the structure of interests. The Basic Interest Scales also were developed to complement the Occupational Scales. The primary difference between the scales is that the Occupational Scales were empirically derived, whereas the Basic Interest Scales were statistically developed to be more homogeneous.

The 1994 SII has 25 Basic Interest Scales, compared with 23 in the previous version. The scales were increased in length to enhance reliability. Some new scales, Computer Activities and Data Management, were added to the Conventional grouping, and two, Culinary Arts and Applied Arts, were added to the Artistic grouping. Two scales were renamed: Business Management became Organizational Management, and Office Practices became Office Services. The Medical Service scale moved from the Investigative area into the Social Service area, and the Athletics scale moved from Social to Realistic.

It is easy to see how, through the examination of the Basic Interest Scales, one can more specifically define what interests underlie the General Occupational Themes, while at the same time achieve a better understanding of the patterns of interests that comprise the Occupational Scales.

The Occupational Scales

The Occupational Scales are the primary base of the 1994 SII, as was true for the SVIB in 1927 and the 1985 SII revision. The 1994 version of the SII contains 211 occupational scales. Fourteen new occupations were added, including actuary, audiologist, auto mechanic, community service organization director, gardener/groundskeeper, medical records technician, technical writer, small business owner, bookkeeper, child care provider, corporate trainer, paralegal, plumber, and translator. Four additional new scales were developed, two for males and two for females, by collapsing the eight groups of military enlistees and the six groups of military officers into Military Enlisted Personnel and Military Officer. Over 46% of the Occupational Scales were based on newly collected data.

Six pairs of scales were renamed to make them more consistent with current occupational titles.

For each occupation, an individual's score is reflected in terms of how similar that individual is to others who are currently employed in the field and who indicate that they are happy in their work. Similarity is reflected on a scale from "Very Dissimilar" to "Very Similar." The occupations in the Occupational Scales also are grouped according to how they fit with the General Occupational Themes.

Summary of Item Responses

The Summary of Item Responses on the 1994 revision of the SII replaces the Administrative Indexes of the 1985 version. This section continues to provide a check of problems in the administration, completion, or scoring of the instrument. These indexes include Total Responses, Infrequent Responses, and the percentage of "Like," "Indifferent," and "Dislike" responses. If the Total Responses Index (TRI) is below 300, the individual interpreting the test should question the accuracy of the results and determine what led to this outcome.

The purpose of the Infrequent Response Index (IRI) is to determine if the answer sheet has been correctly marked. The IRI is composed of items that are selected infrequently or that are uncommon. The highest possible score for men is 8, and for women is 7. If the IRI is below zero or negative, the inventory should be checked for error. Infrequently, individuals may score less than zero and the inventory remains valid. This situation occurs when an individual has unique or uncommon interests.

The "Like" (LP), "Indifferent" (IP), and "Dislike" (DP) percentages of the Administrative Indexes reflect the individual's style in completing the SII. These response percentages are provided for the eight parts of the SII: Occupations, School Subjects, Activities, Leisure Activities, Types of People, Preferences for Activities, Characteristics, and a new section, Work. For Preferences the percentages are expressed as Left, Equivalent, or Right. Also somewhat different than the LP, IP, and DP responses are the "Yes," "Don't Know," and "No" responses given in the Characteristics section.

The normal range of responses for the LP, IP, and DP scales is between 14 and 50. If LP responses are higher, such as 65% on several parts, then the scores on both the General Occupational Themes and the Basic Interest Scales will be inflated. High LP scores, especially in relation to the Occupations section, may reflect the inability to discriminate between items due to lack of awareness of the world of work, or to low self-awareness, or that the individual holds "variety" as a value. In a similar manner, high DP responses may suggest a high level of discrimination and an occupational choice already determined. However, high DP responses do not suggest that the individual really knows how to make a good choice of occupation or career direction. A high percentage of "no" responses to the Characteristics section may indicate problems with self-esteem. When individuals respond with a high percentage of dislikes to the School Subjects section, it may be that the student has had problems with school or the school environment. There may be other responses in the Administrative Indexes that promote counseling professionals to discuss issues with clients, because the SII provides information to assist individuals, but does not provide conclusions without taking other individual characteristics into account.

Introversion-Extroversion

The Introversion-Extroversion scale is effective at discriminating between individuals who prefer working with others and those who would like to work more with things and ideas. This scale reflects an individual's attitude concerning work with other people. Individuals who score 40 or below tend to be more extroverted, and those who score 60 and above generally are more introverted.

The Academic Comfort Scale

The Academic Comfort scale is easily interpreted as indicating an individual's comfort in academic settings. Subsequently, the scale is not a measure of ability, although there is a tendency for those who pursue higher education to score higher on it than those who do not, but it does reflect how much one enjoys being in an academic environment. Sometimes individuals in higher education score quite low on this scale. When this occurs, it may be an indication that the individual looks at education as a means of attaining an occupational goal, even though the process is not positively experienced. Individuals in graduate school tend to score above 50, with the majority scoring between 55 and 60.

Personal Style Scales

The Introversion-Extroversion scale and the Academic Comfort scale of the 1985 SII have been deleted from the 1994 revision. Four new scales have been added, including Work Style, Learning Environment, Leadership Style, and Risk Taking/Adventure.

The Work Style scale differentiates between those individuals who like to work with people and those who prefer to work with ideas, data, or things. Counselors should be aware that the same score reflects different meanings for men and women, and for college students and adults.

The Learning Environment scale identifies those who have significant levels of formal academic education, or practical training and minimal formal academic education. On this scale, scores of about 50 are typical of individuals with bachelor's and master's degrees. Graduates with high school or technical training generally score below 40. People with Ph.D. degrees score approximately 56, while college undergraduate students tend to have average scores below 50.

The Leadership Style scale suggests the leadership role that an individual prefers. The scale provides a continuum that on one extreme suggests individuals who prefer to lead by example and are more comfortable completing tasks themselves, rather than assigning them to others. The other extreme suggests those who are comfortable taking charge and serving as a motivator in directing others.

The Risk Taking/Adventure scale remains similar to the Adventure Basic Interest scale in the Realistic General Occupational Theme area of the 1985 SII. The scale was labeled differently because it seems to indicate a style of working, rather than a particular interest in a certain type of work.

Reliability of the SII

The reliability of the 1985 SII General Occupational Themes has been established over three time periods using test–retest statistics on three different samples. Over a 2-week period a test–retest correlation of .91 was attained. A second study that was conducted over a period of 30 days with a diverse population resulted in a median test–retest correlation of .86. The third study looked at reliability over a 3-year period and resulted in a median test–retest correlation of .81. These results suggest that the General Occupational Themes are relatively stable, but there is some change over time. Similar test–retest correlations for the Basic Interest Scales were determined for the same time periods as reported for the General Occupational Themes. The resulting median test–retest correlations were .91 for 2 weeks, .88 for 30 days, and .82 for 3 years.

The same time periods and samples also were used to determine test–retest reliability for the Occupational Scales. The subsequent results provided median correlations of .92 for the 2-week sample, .89 for the 30-day sample, and .87 for the 3-year sample.

The General Occupational Themes also have been found to have relatively high internal consistency. Median correlations of .92 for males and .91 for females have been reported. Reliability for other scales of the SII can be found in the *Manual of the SVIB-SCII* (Hansen & Campbell, 1985).

The reliability of the 1994 revision of the SII has been enhanced by changing some of the items and by lengthening some of the scales.

Test–retest reliability has been improved by deleting items that were weakly correlated with the existing scales and replacing them with new items that were more highly correlated. When scores from the general reference samples of the 1985 and 1994 General Occupational Theme scales are correlated, the resulting coefficients are .95 for females and .96 for males.

Validity of the SII

As with reliability, validity for the 1985 SII is reported in reference to its specific scales. Construct validity has been established for the General Occupational Themes through comparing them with other tests purported to measure similar interest traits. When the General Occupational Themes of the SII were compared with the scales of the same name on the Vocational Preference Inventory, a median correlation of .765 was obtained, indicating that both inventories measured similar interest traits. A study by Varca and Shaffer (1982) demonstrated that the General Occupational Themes were useful for identifying avocational interests in which individuals choose to participate. Content, concurrent, and predictive validity have been reported for the SII's Basic Interest Scales. Content validity is evident in that each of the Basic Interest Scales reflects an individual's feelings toward a specific set of activities. (Concurrent validity has been established for the Basic Interest Scales as the scores for the occupations range from two to two and one-half standard deviations apart, hence clearly discriminating among different sets of interests. Although the predictive validity of the Basic Interest Scales is not as good as the content or concurrent, there remains support for individual's scores and the occupations they eventually obtain.)

Concurrent validity has been established for the Occupational Scales through comparing criterion samples (occupations) and reference samples (men and women), and by comparing the mean scores of occupations on each other's scales. The overlap for the criterion and reference samples was reported as 36%, less than two standard deviations on the average. The mean scores for various occupations on different Occupational Scales ranged three to four standard deviations. Numerous studies have been performed that report predictive validity for the SII and its earlier versions. Most of these studies support Strong's (1935) initial belief that measured interests are predictive of occupational choice.

The item content of the 1994 SII revision remains consistent with the 1985 edition to maintain content and construct validity. Because the revised General Occupational Themes for the 1994 SII have demonstrated improved reliability, the authors suggest it is reasonable to expect that the scales also would demonstrate improved validity. The new *Strong*

Interest Inventory Applications and Technical Guide (Harmon, Hansen, Borgen, & Hammer, 1994) provides tables to evaluate construct and content validity based on occupational differences and academic majors. The authors of the *Guide* state the necessity of future studies to confirm the expected validity of the 1994 revision of the SII.

Advantages and Disadvantages of the SII

Isaacson (1985) has identified five advantages and four disadvantages of the Strong-Campbell Interest Inventory (SCII), the earlier version of the SII. The advantages include:

1. The SCII is considered a paragon in the psychometric field. Its stature has grown over its half-century of use.
2. The manual, with its vast statistical base, has long been recognized as excellent.
3. Data from the profile form are provided at three levels: broad and general on the General Theme Scales, cluster or group on the Basic Interest Scales, and occupationally specific on the Occupational Scales.
4. Follow-up data from earlier forms provide powerful evidence of test validity.
5. Most people can complete the form in a short time and with little difficulty or confusion.

The disadvantages include:

1. Centralized scoring requires an inevitable delay, usually of a week or more, before results are available. (This disadvantage has been negated with the new on-site computer scoring.)
2. Individual response style affects the scores. The individual with few like responses may be highly certain of his or her preferences and have a very specific, firmly established career orientation, or on the other hand may be very passive, dependent, and uncertain.
3. Inconsistencies that are confusing to clients can appear between basic interest scores and occupational scales.
4. The present SCII is based on data from occupational samples collected at an earlier time; hence scores for young women whose education has included less emphasis on traditional sex-role stereotypes may be unfairly compared with scores of more traditional women.

The 1994 revision of the SII is based on a sample of more than 60,000 men and women. The sample is more ethnically diverse than any previous sample with representation from all socioeconomic and educational backgrounds.

The Case of Lisa

"Lisa Biggs" was a 21-year-old full-time student majoring in advertising. She was an unmarried senior currently employed part-time in telemarketing with previous experience in retail sales and waitressing who had become aware that she did not want to pursue a major in advertising. Lisa's primary concern was that she was just not as competitive or oriented toward making her career a primary life endeavor, as many of her fellow students were inclined to do. In order to determine what other occupational areas might be of interest to her, the SCII, the predecessor to the SII, was administered. The primary challenge was to find another occupational area that was compatible with Lisa's interests that would not require many additional hours of college education.

Strong-Campbell Interest Inventory Results

Academic Comfort 44
Introversion-Extroversion 46

Themes:
Social	61
Artistic	58
Investigative	50
Conventional	47
Realistic	45
Enterprising	38

Basic Interest Scales:

Very High:	Adventure	63
High:	Art	64
	Religious Activities	64
Moderately High:	Music/Dramatics	61
	Social Service	60
	Domestic Arts	62
	Law/Politics	56
Moderately Low:	Nature	43
	Medical Science	43
	Merchandising	39
	Business Management	38

Occupations:

Similar:	Police Officer	45
	Art Teacher	48
	Musician	45
	Flight Attendant	51
	Advertising Executive	45
	Special Education Teacher	48

(continued)

29

Moderately Similar:	Photographer 42
	Broadcaster 43
	Guidance Counselor 42
	Elementary Teacher 44
	Occupational Therapist 41
	Dental Hygienist 44
	YMCA/YWCA Director 42
	Funeral Director 40

Administrative Scales:			
Occupations	47 L%	5 I%	48 D%
School Subjects	58 L%	0 I%	42 D%
Activities	61 L%	2 I%	37 D%
Leisure Activities	46 L%	0 I%	54 D%
Types of People	58 L%	0 I%	42 D%
Characteristics	57 Y%	21 ?%	21 N%

The Administrative Indexes for Lisa's results suggested rather well-defined preferences, large numbers of Like (L) percentages and Dislike (D) percentages, and low percentages of Indifferent (I) percentages. However, she did indicate "Like" for nearly half of the occupations, 47%, and over half of the school subjects, 58%. In addition, although there was some differentiation between the General Occupational Themes, five of the themes were within six points of each other, producing a relatively flat profile. This response set led to questions about what she had done to choose her major, to which she responded that she simply liked art. She had not had any formal assistance in making her choice of major, nor had she utilized many resources for career exploration. Lisa had perceived advertising as a way to pursue her artistic interests and make a good living. Through the interview and the use of additional assessment instruments in the C-DAC battery, it was determined that the conflicts for Lisa were related to values. She was worried that she would have to relocate away from her family and did not like the competitive nature of the advertising world that was being reflected in her classes.

In attempting to help Lisa, we examined the General Occupational Themes, and found Social to be moderately high. The four themes that followed Social in strength were Artistic, Investigative, Conventional, and Realistic. With her scores highest in relation to Social and Artistic General Occupational Themes, it was not surprising to find that most of the occupations that were most "Similar" for Lisa also were in these two areas. The Basic Interest Scales provided some help, as Lisa verified interests largely in relation to Art and Social Service occupations. As for Adventure, she explained that she enjoyed taking risks, but more in relation to leisure activities than to her occupation. As Lisa had indicated that she liked such a large number of occupations, school subjects, activities, leisure activities, etc., the SCII also reflected many occupations that were "Similar" or "Moderately Similar."

The overall analysis of the SII, combined with the counseling interview, suggested that Lisa may have not been ready to make a decision concerning her career. She contracted to do additional work in relation to exploring options, and to participate in activities that would assist her in gaining a better understanding of herself. As her Academic Comfort score indicated that she was relatively at ease in an academic environment, graduate school was discussed as a means of giving herself more time to determine exactly what she wanted to do and to remain productive at the same time. Upon termination, Lisa was heavily leaning toward elementary education with specialization in teaching art, although she had not yet completed her exploration activities.

THE VALUES SCALE

The Values Scale (VS) was developed by Dorothy Nevill and Donald E. Super (1989a) as part of the International Work Importance Study (WIS). The WIS brought together psychologists from Europe, North America, Australia, Asia, and Africa who were interested in the values and satisfactions that people pursue in work and other life roles.

The objective of the WIS was to determine the importance of one's work role in relation to other life roles, and how values influence these roles. Super had developed an earlier inventory to assess values, the Work Values Inventory (1970), but it had the limitations of not addressing some significant values, and some of its scales were not as reliable as would be desired. Subsequently, the VS was developed to measure intrinsic and extrinsic values. The focus of the VS included both general and work-related values.

To determine which values would be addressed in the VS, researchers from England and the United States involved in the WIS conducted a literature review to develop a values list that was then reviewed by research teams in other countries. The next step was for the various teams to write definitions for each value. Further refinement was accomplished with pilot studies where item-scale correlations and item-factor analyses were calculated for the samples. When the WIS research teams pooled their results, a number of scales were dropped due to interitem correlation between scales. Numerous discussions and revisions followed that resulted in the list of 21 values currently utilized in the VS (see Table 2.2). Finally, pilot studies were conducted that tested the items on small samples.

One of the major issues addressed in the development of the VS was related to measuring life and work values with the same instrument. The

TABLE 2.2 The Values Scale Definitions

Values	Sample Statements
1. Ability Utilization	Use all my skills and knowledge
2. Achievement	Have results that show that I have done well
3. Advancement	Get ahead
4. Aesthetics	Make life more beautiful
5. Altruism	Help people with problems
6. Authority	Tell others what to do
7. Autonomy	Act on my own
8. Creativity	Discover, develop, or design new things
9. Economic Rewards	Have a high standard of living
10. Life Style	Live according to my own ideas
11. Personal Development	Develop as a person
12. Physical Activity	Get a lot of exercise
13. Prestige	Be admired for my knowledge and skills
14. Risk	Do risky things
15. Social Interaction	Do things with other people
16. Social Relations	Be with friends
17. Variety	Have every day be different in some way from the one before it
18. Working Conditions	Have good space and light in which to work
19. Cultural Identity	Live where people of my religion and race are accepted
20. Physical Prowess	Work hard physically
21. Economic Security	Be where employment is regular and secure

question is often raised as to whether values can be separated between work and life in general. To address this issue, the research teams involved in the WIS utilized five trial items representing general values at the beginning of each test booklet, and five items representing specific work content in the second half of the booklet. The structures of the scales representing general life values and work values were very similar. The final version of the VS was reduced to five items for each value to facilitate test administration. Of these five items, two represent work-related values, two represent general life values, and the final item was selected due to its empirical strength.

Reliability

According to the manual for the VS (Nevill & Super, 1989b), two measures of reliability were determined: internal consistency (alpha coefficients) and stability (test–retest). The alpha coefficients for the VS items were generally above .70 for samples of high school students, college students, and adults. Test–retest reliabilities were sampled only for the college student population, and the resulting correlations were less than .70 for several scales. A second test–retest study was conducted on a larger population with similar results.

Validity

Content and construct validity were assessed for the VS. Predictive validity has not been established as the instrument is relatively new and there has not been sufficient time to conduct longitudinal studies. One study, however, conducted by Krau (1989), supported that subjects belonging to either high or low socioeconomic status maintain an unbroken transition in work values as the various social groups moved from high school into the role of adult worker.

Content validity was established through examining the content of items for face validity, reviewing the methods used to develop the items, and the item-scale correlations. Teams of specialists from different countries wrote the items according to agreed upon definitions. The methods used to identify the items included literature reviews from each of the participating countries, eliminating items that had similar meanings, utilizing researchers of various nationalities to write definitions for the values, and continual refinement of the definitions of values as researchers from various countries met together. The definition of each value was developed by researchers from at least two different countries to ensure generalizability. Item selection was accomplished through item-scale correlations and factor analytic procedures to assure internal consistency and scale independence. Some scales, however, had significant intercorrelations.

Construct validity was established through the examination of normative mean differences for values between males and females, and through factor structure. It was found that there were more differences between males and females in terms of which values were preferred in high school than in college or adulthood. As educational level and age increased, there was less propensity for sex-stereotypic values to exist. This finding provides evidence that supports construct validity for the VS.

Another supporting element for construct validity of the VS related to the finding that eight of the value scales factored into the same six factors for all samples: high school, college, and adult. The six factors were Prestige, Risk, Cultural Identity, Creativity, Social Interaction, and Social Relations. Other factors were different across the three samples in a way that seemed consistent with maturation. Examples of these factors included Economics, Life Style, Personal Development, Physical Activity, and Physical Prowess. The last evidence supporting construct validity was the finding that the factor structure of the VS was similar in samples of students from different countries (Lokan, 1983; Sverko, 1982).

Shears (1982) provided additional support for the construct validity of the VS with his findings of positive correlations between the Work Aspect Preference Scale (WAPS) (Pryor, 1981) and the VS. Shears also found high positive correlations between the Work Quiz (Taylor, 1975) and the VS. Yates (1990a) investigated the construct validity of the VS and determined that it was useful in the assessment of work-related values.

Administration and Scoring

The VS is available in seven different languages and has norms for Americans, Canadians, Yugoslavians, and Portuguese. The VS has 105 scored items that yield 21 separate scales. It is appropriate for administration to high school students, college students, and adults, taking between 30 and 45 minutes for completion.

The reading level for the VS is established approximately at the eighth grade. Although there is considerable demographic information requested, only the sex and some identification for each subject are required for scoring. For each of the 105 items there are four possible responses:

1—of little or no importance
2—of some importance
3—important
4—very important

The VS either may be mailed to the publisher for scoring, be computer scored, or be hand scored. For each value there are five items with a potential value of four, providing for a possible total of 20. There is one extra item, making the total 106 items, that is only used when scoring the VS for cross-national studies. Local percentile norms are available from the publisher when 100 or more cases are scored. High school, college, and adult norms are available in the 1989 edition of the VS manual.

The Case of Lisa Revisited

Lisa Biggs, who we discussed earlier in the presentation on the SII, was a 21-year-old female who was in her senior year of college majoring in advertising. She was employed part-time in telemarketing. Lisa became concerned about the level of competition in advertising and that she found classes in her major less enjoyable as she progressed through her program. She also was concerned that she was not as aggressive as others in her major, and did not have the same level of enthusiasm for her occupational alternatives as her peers. By the time Lisa entered counseling, she had already determined that she did not want to pursue advertising as a career. Lisa was administered the VS as part of her career counseling.

The Values Scale (Ratings Range from 1 = Low to 4 = High)

4.0 . . . . . Achievement
3.8 . . . . . Ability Utilization
3.4 . . . . . Creativity
3.4 . . . . . Personal Development
3.2 . . . . . Prestige
3.2 . . . . . Social Relations
3.2 . . . . . Economic Security
2.8 . . . . . Advancement
2.8 . . . . . Economic Rewards
2.8 . . . . . Working Conditions
2.6 . . . . . Aesthetics
2.6 . . . . . Life Style
2.6 . . . . . Social Interaction
2.4 . . . . . Altruism
2.4 . . . . . Cultural Identity
2.2 . . . . . Variety
2.0 . . . . . Authority
2.0 . . . . . Physical Activity
1.8 . . . . . Autonomy
1.2 . . . . . Physical Prowess
1.2 . . . . . Risk

Lisa's highest rated values were Achievement, Ability Utilization, Creativity, Personal Development, Prestige, Social Relations, and Economic Security, which all tend to be more intrinsic in nature than extrinsic. Although many of her preferred values were compatible with advertising, she was concerned with economic security and having to relocate to find a position, which meant leaving her friends and family. As the counseling interview progressed, Lisa expressed that her interests in advertising were largely related to creativity, one of her most important values.

Her later decision to pursue a career as an elementary teacher reflected Lisa's values as identified on the VS. She indicated that all of her most important values were positively addressed in pursuing a major in elementary education with an emphasis in art. This choice allowed Lisa to remain close to her friends and family, and would provide economic security. She also could utilize her abilities through this choice, be creative and admired for her performance, and demonstrate that she could do well as an elementary teacher.

THE SALIENCE INVENTORY

The SI was developed by Dorothy Nevill and Donald Super as part of the international WIS mentioned earlier. The SI was designed for use with students and adults as a measure of the life space aspects of the Life Career Rainbow (Super, 1980, 1990). As noted by Zytowski (1988), the concepts and verbal representations within the SI reflect the "different perspectives of agnostic, Catholic, and Protestant nations, of Capitalist, Socialist, and Communist economies, and of developed and developing nations of North America, Europe, and Asia" (p. 152). The SI was created in order to measure the relative importance of five life roles: student, worker, citizen, homemaker, and leisurite. More specifically, the SI assesses the level of participation and commitment to each of these life roles as well as the associated values expectations within each role. The SI is available in the languages of 13 countries on five continents.

Reliability and Validity

Two measures of reliability are reported in the manual for the SI (Nevill & Super, 1986a): internal consistency (alpha coefficients) for high school, college, and adults samples; and stability (test–retest) for the college population. The alphas were above .80 for all three populations. Niles, Sowa, and Laden (1994) reported Cronbach alphas ranging from .80 to .90 for SI. Test–retest correlations for the Participation and Commitment scales range from .59 to .83. The range for the Values Expectations scale is .37 (leisure activities) to .67 with a median r of .58.

Content and construct validity have been assessed for the SI. The need for content validity was an intrinsic part of the development of the SI. Teams of specialists from different countries met in small groups and plenary meetings in order to refine the definitions of life roles and "Which values do you seek" (in each of the five life roles). The SI yields 15 scores (five role scores for each of the three dimensions). Response options are:

1— "Never" or "Rarely," and "Little" or "None"
2— "Sometimes" and "Some"

3— "Often" and "Quite a Lot"
4— "Almost Always" or "Always" and "A Great Deal"

The SI requires approximately 30 to 45 minutes to administer and is appropriate for high school, college, and adult populations. It may be either mailed to the publisher for scoring or be hand scored.

The Case of Jonathan

Jonathan, a 27-year-old male, came to the career center in order to receive assistance in making a decision related to whether or not he should pursue a graduate degree in social work. He was in his last semester of undergraduate study and had majored in psychology. Jonathan expressed an interest in working as a counselor with adolescents. His values, interests, and skills appeared to be appropriate for the helping professions, so on one level this program of study (social work) was a good option for him. However, as he talked with his counselor, it became apparent that some of the difficulty Jonathan was having in making his decision related to lifestyle concerns. That is, as the father of a 2-year-old daughter, Jonathan was committed to actively being involved in the parenting role. He also was very active in church activities and spent many hours teaching Sunday school and directing a youth group. Jonathan wanted to be certain that his future career options allowed for his continued participation in these activities.

The results of the SI (see Figure 2.2) reinforced Jonathan's statements about his participation and commitment in the life roles of homemaker (home and family), citizen (community activities), and leisurite. His participation scores for these three life roles were 3.8, 3.6, and 3.6, respectively. The commitment scores were similar (4.0, 3.8, and 3.8, respectively).

Of additional interest were Jonathan's SI results related to the worker role. For this life role, his participation score was 3.1, his commitment score was 2.8, and his values expectations score was 2.6. In discussing this score, Jonathan felt that the relatively low commitment and values expectations scores (in both cases, these scores were more than one standard deviation below the mean for other adult males) were reflections of his perception that his occupational pursuits inevitably would infringe on his other life roles. This led to a discussion of Jonathan's career beliefs (e.g., how much time he would need to spend "on the job" to perform at an acceptable level, what his career and life goals were). It became apparent during this discussion that Jonathan was lacking in occupational information with regard to his preferred occupation and with regard to the helping professions in general. Given this, considerable time was spent accumulating information related to a wide range of helping occupations that would allow him to achieve his stated career goal (counseling adolescents).

FIGURE 2.2   Report Form for The Salience Inventory

Report Form for the Salience Inventory

Donald E. Super, Ph.D. and Dorothy D. Nevill, Ph.D.

Name __JONATHAN__   Age __27__ Sex __M__ Education _____   Marital Status __M__   Date _____

Occupational Status _____

Occupational Group _____

Status Satisfaction
  Student _____
  Occupation _____
  Leisure _____
  Community Inv. _____

Occupational Level
  Self _____
  Father _____
  Mother _____
  Spouse _____

Scales	Total Score	Total Score
Participation[1]		
Studying	31	
Working	36	
Community Service	38	
Home and Family	36	
Leisure Activities		
Commitment[1]		
Studying	28	
Working	38	
Community Service	40	
Home and Family	38	
Leisure Activities		
Value Expectations[2]		
Studying	42	
Working	37	
Community Service	48	
Home and Family	55	
Leisure Activities	48	

[1] To get average, divide total score by 10.
[2] To get average, divide total score by 14.

Fill in the average score for each category.

	Study	Work	Com.	H&F	Leisure	Total
Part.	3.0	3.1	3.6	3.8	3.6	
Com.	2.9	2.8	3.8	4.0	3.8	
V.E.	3.0	2.6	3.4	3.9	3.4	
Total						

See reverse side of page for comparative means and standard deviations.

After reviewing the information he had gathered in light of his interests, skills, values, and goals, Jonathan came to the conclusion that school counseling would provide him with the best opportunity to achieve his career goal, while at the same time providing him with opportunities to participate in the life roles to which he was committed (i.e., parenting and community service).

AN INTEGRATION OF INSTRUMENTS INTO THE C-DAC BATTERY

Described in detail in this chapter have been the five assessment instruments that comprise the C-DAC battery: the Strong Interest Inventory, the Career Development Inventory appropriate for adolescents and college students or the Adult Career Concerns Inventory for adults, The Values Scale, and The Salience Inventory. Below is a sample profile of results from these assessments for a 26-year-old, divorced woman reentering the work force who sought career counseling at a university counseling center.

C-DAC Assessment Results:

Career Development Inventory
(College Form)

(Percentile Scores)

Career Planning	18
Career Exploration	86
Decision-Making	83
World-of-Work Information	89
Career Development Attitudes	57
Career Development Knowledge	92
Career Orientation Total	82
Knowledge of Preferred Occupation	55

Strong Interest Inventory

Academic Comfort	53
Introversion-Extroversion	48

Themes:

Investigative	60
Conventional	55
Artistic	53
Enterprising	52
Realistic	45
Social	44

(continued)

Basic Interest Scales:
  Very High: None
  Moderately High: Business Management 60
                      Merchandising 59
                      Sales 55
                      Science, Mathematics 56
                      Mechanical 55

Occupations:
  Very Similar: Marketing Executive 48
                      Restaurant Manager 46
                      Purchasing Agent 45
  Similar: IRS Agent 52
  Moderately Similar: Systems Analyst 51
                      R & D Manager 43
                      Optometrist 42
                      Investment Manager 43
                      Optician 41

The Values Scale

(Ratings Range from 1 = Low to 4 = High)

    3.6 .... Personal Development
    3.6 .... Working Conditions
    3.4 .... Ability Utilization
    3.4 .... Prestige
    3.4 .... Creativity
    3.4 .... Aesthetics
    3.2 .... Achievement
    3.2 .... Advancement
    3.2 .... Economic Rewards
    3.2 .... Life Style
    3.2 .... Autonomy
    3.2 .... Economic Security
    3.0 .... Variety
    2.6 .... Authority
    2.0 .... Altruism
    2.0 .... Social Relations
    1.8 .... Physical Activity
    1.8 .... Physical Prowess
    1.4 .... Social Interaction
    1.2 .... Cultural Identity
    1.2 .... Risk

(continued)

The Salience Inventory

(Ratings Range from 1 = Low to 4 = High)

	Study	Work	Community Service	Home & Family	Leisure Activities
Participation	3.6	3.4	1.1	3.1	2.8
Commitment	3.2	3.5	1.6	3.6	3.1
Values Expectations	2.9	2.4	1.2	2.9	2.8

Super et al. (1992) suggest two possible orders in which the C-DAC instruments can be analyzed and interpreted. The first order begins with the CDI (or ACCI), then proceeds to the SII, the VS, and SI. The rationale for this order is that an assessment of career maturity (from the CDI) is necessary for the counselor to establish how much confidence can be placed in the remaining self-assessments, and whether career decision making should be encouraged or delayed. In other words, if an adolescent or college student has poor career planning and exploration attitudes and knows little about the world of work, would he or she be able to know what he or she likes and dislikes on an interest inventory? Furthermore, would that student have a clear picture of his or her values and how they could be achieved in the various life roles? If not, career and self-exploration should become the immediate focus of counseling, rather than career decision making. With adults, the ACCI first gives the counselor a look at the developmental tasks that the client is focused on, then moves to the interests that the client expresses (SII), the values that underlie those interests (VS), and the relative importance of the life roles in which the client seeks the fulfillment of those interests and values (SI) (Super et al., 1992, p. 77).

In the sample profile above, the CDI scales indicate that this woman has an overall high career maturity score (82nd percentile), compared to college freshmen, and thus the counselor should test the assumption that this client knows herself fairly well, and has an adequate amount of information about the world of work to be able to specify a clear direction of interests and values. On the other hand, this client has not been planful about her career development to date (18th percentile on the Career Planning scale) and knows only an average amount of information about the career area in which she says she has an interest (Business: Sales and Promotion) (55th percentile). Thus, the client should be encouraged to acquire more specific career information before deciding on a major in business.

The second order suggested by Super et al. (1992) begins with the SII, followed by the VS, the CDI/ACCI, and the SI. The rationale for beginning with the SII is more pragmatic: Most clients are enthusiastic about receiving their results from the SII because many come to counseling to find or confirm an occupational choice (Super et al., 1992, p. 77). The process continues with the assessment of values underlying the interests, relative importance of life roles, as well as career maturity. In light of the career maturity scores, "it is then possible to ask whether the interest inventory scores may be taken as indexes of wise choices or should be viewed as signs of what might be good fields of activity to explore and to try out before making a choice" (Super et al., 1992, p. 77). In addition, beginning with the SII meets the client where he or she is and encourages the client's motivation to continue with the process of career counseling.

The C-DAC battery has multiple uses in career counseling. For adult clients, the ACCI helps the counselor pinpoint the current level of client concern in each of Super's career development stages. It also helps the client anticipate future career concerns that he or she is likely to encounter. The assessment of current concerns stimulates the counseling question, "For each of these concerns, what will be necessary for you to successfully deal with these concerns?" In addition, "For those career stages that you will confront in the future, how can you be best prepared to handle them successfully?"

In the case of adolescents, who are primarily concerned with the developmental tasks of exploration, the CDI allows the counselor to assess the client's developmental level of career maturity, possibly calling into question the results from the remaining assessments. In these cases, the career maturity information from the CDI scales helps the counselor suggest counseling goals for the client, such as obtaining more information about the world of work, a specific area of interest, or coping with barriers that have prevented the client from exploration activities. Increasing career maturity, then, becomes the immediate focus of counseling, rather than making a career decision.

The SII assesses the vocational and avocational interests that one has developed as a result of interaction with the environment. Exploration of the environment facilitates the clarification of interests and the integration of those interests into the self-concept. In the sample case above, the client has acquired general information about the world of work and knows an average amount about Business: Sales and Promotion through interaction with the environment. However, her interest profile is fairly undifferentiated; her scores on Investigative, Conventional, Artistic, and Enterprising are virtually interchangeable. Upon examining her occupational scale scores, there is some evidence to support her interest in business occupations, but her interest in science should also be investigated further.

The VS assesses the work and non-work-related values that underlie interests. That is, what are the values that one hopes to realize through engaging in activities associated with his or her interests? Our sample client above places the highest value on personal development and working conditions. Which of her interest areas provide opportunities for these values to be met? And which of her interest areas will not involve her lowest value, social interaction, or working with other people? If she does indeed want to avoid social interaction, then many Business: Sales and Promotion jobs would not be suitable. However, she may be more attracted to those sales occupations that involve indirect sales, rather than direct.

Finally, the SI gives the counselor some indication of the life roles in which the client hopes to realize his or her values and interests. The client above appears to be actively involved in her study, work, and home/family roles. She also has the greatest emotional attachment to the home/family, work, and then study roles. The study, home/family, and leisure roles seem to loom large in her future. The importance of work drops off in her future expectations. In which of these life roles does she expect to meet her high values and avoid her low ones? In which of these life roles would she like to engage in activities related to her inventoried interests?

With the assessment of developmental level and cumulative information that the C-DAC battery provides, the counselor can generate hypotheses to be checked out with the client that will stimulate rich counseling material. For example, in the sample case above, the counselor also might notice that the client's values expectations scores from the SI drop off in all of the life roles. The counselor might hypothesize that this is due to the client's confusion as to which of the life roles will be most rewarding in her future. This would not be unexpected because the client is recently divorced and is most likely in a state of crisis or, at least, flux. Another hypothesis might be that since (a) the client places fairly low value on social interaction, (b) she is in the average range on introversion-extroversion, and (c) her highest General Occupational Theme score is Investigative, her career aspiration of a business occupation in sales or promotions may be more motivated by her current financial needs rather than her interests and values.

The C-DAC model of career counseling should stimulate many interesting research questions. For example, Super (1992) suggests that research is needed on the sequencing of the assessments and on the process of career counseling with the battery of assessments. Research also should focus on the C-DAC model's effectiveness compared to more traditional models of career counseling. For example, Super (personal communication, February 2, 1989) hypothesized that use of the C-DAC model with students who have low career maturity might result in expanded information-gathering activity, increased use of career decision-making treatments, and clearer interests. He also hypothesized that students with low study or work commitment scores might develop more "specific, congruent, and stable occupational preferences, curricular choices, and career plans" if provided with a C-DAC interpretation. Super was especially interested in the relationship between career maturity and salience scores with interest inventory scores and occupational stability and satisfaction.

Data collection on special populations (adults in career transition, college students, minority high school students) has begun at several research sites, including the University of Virginia, the University of North Carolina at Greensboro, the University of Georgia, and Austin, Texas, and should be encouraged. Although there are isolated studies of minority respondents on each of the C-DAC instruments, more comprehensive data on the full battery for culturally diverse respondents are needed. Some career development research questions that could be addressed by these kinds of data are: "Is career maturity related to interest pattern structure and work salience in the same ways for Hispanics, Blacks, and Caucasians?," "How are specific values related to salience of life roles within culturally diverse groups?," "How does the salience of work fluctuate with clients' stages of career development, and does this differ for members of diverse populations?"

So far this book has presented information about the theoretical foundation of the C-DAC approach, the test instruments that make it up, and how they come together to assist career counseling. The next three chapters describe how the approach can be used with adolescents, college students, and adults.

3

Developmental Career Counseling With Adolescents

The theoretical basis of developmental career counseling with adolescents is presented first in this chapter, followed by a discussion of Donald E. Super's developmental model of career counseling. Three case studies are then used to demonstrate the Career Development, Assessment, and Counseling (C-DAC) approach.

THE THEORETICAL BASIS

According to Super, Thompson, Lindeman, Jordaan, and Myers (1988a), adolescents are confronting the developmental tasks of the Exploration stage of career development; that is, they are most concerned with "crystallizing" their ideas about what line of work they would be best suited for, "specifying" the most suitable career alternative from those considered possible, and "implementing" some initial plans to get started in their chosen careers. Thus, counselors could expect adolescents to score highest on the Exploration stage as assessed by the Adult Career Concerns Inventory (ACCI; Super et al., 1988a), and to not indicate much concern regarding the future stages of career development (Establishment, Maintenance, and Disengagement). Although rigid age limits are not associated with the Exploration stage (for example, concern with exploration reoccurs as adults face layoffs and self-initiated career changes), Super suggests that exploratory tasks are predominant among 15 to 25 year olds. Adolescents must successfully confront the tasks of this exploration stage in order to navigate the challenges of the next stage of career development, Establishment, or becoming entrenched in one's chosen field or occupation.

Super theorizes that in order for adolescents to successfully confront the Exploration stage of career development, they must possess "career maturity," a complex, multidimensional construct that has attitudinal and cognitive (knowledge-based) components. Attitudinal components of career maturity include such career planning and exploration attitudes as thoughtfulness and planfulness about one's career development, the willingness to utilize a variety of sources of information for career exploration, and to find these sources of information useful. Cognitive or knowledge components include knowledge of career development principles, the ability to apply these principles to particular career decisions, knowledge of the occupational structure and what it takes to get and keep a job, and knowledge of one's particular field of interest. Career maturity also implies autonomy and a sense of being in control of one's destiny, a realistic perspective on one's career possibilities in light of one's strengths and limitations, a time perspective that allows for reflection on the past and anticipation of the future, high self-esteem, and good decision-making skills (Super, 1983). The degree of career maturity is presumed to affect the quality of decision making at each developmental stage (Osipow, 1990). In other words, possessing a greater degree of career maturity at the Exploration stage of career development should lead to more appropriate initial career-related behaviors and decisions.

More specifically, the attitudinal elements of career maturity include thoughtfulness and planfulness about one's career development, the willingness to engage in exploratory behaviors (such as talking to teachers, school counselors, and significant others; using occupational information; and talking with people currently in the school or occupation one is considering), and the ability to make use of various sources of information. The cognitive components of career maturity include knowledge of the world of work, one's chosen field of interest, and career decision-making principles. Knowledge of the world of work would include, for example, the adolescent's knowledge of how physicians and mail carriers learn their jobs and what equipment medical laboratory technicians and stock brokers use. Knowledge of one's field of interest would include, for example, knowing what abilities and interests are compatible with one's currently preferred occupation. Knowledge of career decision-making principles would include knowledge of which career factors should be given priority in particular decision scenarios.

Counselors can use the Career Development Inventory—School Form (CDI; Super, Thompson, Lindeman, Jordaan, & Myers, 1979) to assess the degree of adolescents' attitudinal and cognitive career maturity. In particular, the attitudinal scales (Career Planning [CP] and Career Exploration [CE]) measure planfulness about one's career development and the willingness to engage in career exploration, respectively; the cognitive scales are Decision-Making [DM], World-of-Work Information [WW], and Knowledge of Preferred Occupation [PO] assess one's knowledge of career decision-making principles, what it takes to get a job and succeed in the world of work, and knowledge of one's preferred occupation, respectively. It is important to note that Part II of the instrument, which is scored to obtain the PO scale score, should not be administered to students below the 11th grade, because these items require knowledge that younger students are not likely to possess. Data from the high school sample upon which the CDI was normed show a pattern of increasing career maturity from the 9th to the 11th grade, with a slight decrease in the 12th grade (Super, Thompson, Lindeman, Jordaan, & Myers, 1988c, p. 23). Perhaps this reflects a decrease in concern with exploration during the final year of high school because by this time at least some preliminary decisions about work and college have usually been made.

It is important to note that the Decision-Making scale of the CDI should be interpreted with caution because there is some evidence to suggest that high scores on this scale are not correlated highly with the ability to make appropriate decisions for oneself (Westbrook, Sanford, & Donnelly, 1990). Therefore, the Decision-Making scale is more appropriately interpreted as "knowledge of career decision-making principles."

Counselors can use the scores from the CDI to ascertain if low career maturity reflects an attitudinal problem, a cognitive problem, or both. If attitudinal scores are low, then counseling interventions need to be directed at developing positive career planning and exploration attitudes. The issues at the root of unwillingness to explore or lack of thoughtfulness about one's career should be investigated. If the CDI cognitive scale scores are low, then efforts need to be made toward increasing the adolescent's knowledge-base about the world of work, the currently preferred field of interest, or both. On the other hand, if career maturity scores are high, the positive coping behaviors that produced these high scores should be identified and the adolescent reinforced for engaging in such behaviors.

In addition to utilizing the information that the CDI provides, counselors should informally assess some additional factors that are implied by the notion of "career maturity." Possessing good decision-making skills is considered crucial to successfully confronting the tasks of the Exploration stage of career development, especially the ability to develop alternatives and make some initial selections from these alternatives. Future time perspective also has been demonstrated to be an important element in effective career decision making (Super, Starishevsky, Matlin, & Jordaan, 1963, as cited in Herr & Cramer, 1992, p. 195; Savickas, Silling, & Schwartz, 1984); an adolescent needs to have a concern with the future and his or her role in it. And, lastly, realism is an important dimension of career maturity (Super, 1990). "This is a mixed affective and cognitive entity best assessed by combining personal, self-report, and objective data, as in comparing the aptitudes of the individual with the aptitudes typical of people in the occupation to which he or she aspires" (Super, 1990, p. 213). Thus, the counselor should ask (a) does the adolescent project a concern with his or her future role in the world of work, (b) is he or she able to generate realistic alternatives, given his or her assets, weaknesses, limitations, and opportunities, and (c) does the adolescent have the decision-making skills to be able to select from those realistic alternatives some initial career-seeking behaviors that will lead to an appropriate career direction? Deficiencies in any of these areas could suggest appropriate counseling goals.

Vocational interests are a primary determinant of satisfying career choices, that is, choices congruent with interests tend to be more satisfying than those that are not (Holland, 1985). Although there is much still to be learned about the development of vocational interests, the direction in which these interests tend to lie can be understood in the context of social learning theory. Bandura (1977) posited that behavior, personal factors, and environmental factors "operate as interlocking determinants of each other" (p. 10). Cognitions play a mediating role in translating environmental influences into behavior (Mitchell & Krumboltz, 1990).

The basic proposition of social learning theory is that behavior is the result of "unique learning experiences, rather than innate developmental or psychic processes. These learning experiences consist of contact with and cognitive analysis of positively and negatively reinforcing events" (Mitchell & Krumboltz, 1990, p. 145). A complex interaction of genetic predispositions, environmental conditions and events, unique learning experiences, and resulting task approach skills produce certain cognitions, beliefs, skills, and actions relevant to one's career choices and decision making, including self-observations about one's vocational interests typically assessed by some type of interest inventory. Thus, inventoried vocational interests can be conceptualized as self-observation generalizations resulting from past learning experiences. These self-observation generalizations in turn influence one's career choices.

Holland (1985) also takes a social learning approach to the development of vocational interests. His basic proposition is that "types produce types" (p. 11). He argues that parental types provide certain environmental opportunities and deficits that influence the child's direction of vocational interests. He provides the example of Realistic parents who surround themselves with tools and equipment in the home, select Realistic friends, and also tend to reject Social activities and situations. However, he incorporates the concept of reciprocal determinism, recognizing that children exert influence on their environments as well.

To summarize how interests develop, within environments that provide certain opportunities and reinforcements depending on the types dominating the environments,

> a child's special heredity and experience first lead to preferences for
> some kinds of activities and aversions to others. Later, these preferences

become well-defined interests from which the person gains self-satisfaction as well as reward from others. Still later, the pursuit of these interests leads to the development of more specialized competencies as well as to the neglect of other potential competencies. At the same time, a person's differentiation of interests with age is accompanied by a crystallization of correlated values. (Holland, 1985, p. 12)

And thus, personality types are formed.

Super et al. (1992) advocate the use of the Strong Interest Inventory (SII; Hansen & Campbell, 1985), "one of the most widely used and best validated of career assessment measures" (p. 75), to ascertain the general direction in which an adolescent's interests tend to lie. It yields standard scores on the six Holland types: Realistic, Investigative, Artistic, Social, Enterprising, and Conventional. Also, Basic Interest Scales yield scores on 23 fields of work, and an adolescent's pattern of interests is compared with those of satisfied workers in 207 occupations. The 1994 revision of the SII yields scores on 25 Basic Interest Scales and compares a respondent's profile to satisfied workers in 211 occupations. Furthermore, the SII provides information on an adolescent's preference for working with people, things, or ideas (Introversion-Extroversion scale), and on interests in practical versus theoretical pursuits (Academic Comfort scale). Counselors can use the SII to help an adolescent clarify his or her interests, to suggest occupations for further exploration, and as a springboard to brainstorm additional occupations with similar features to the profiled ones. Related to this last point, because the occupations profiled on the SII are a small sample of approximately 20,000 occupations available in the United States, those on the SII that the adolescent finds appealing should be used to generate additional occupations with similar characteristics that the adolescent may wish to explore.

It is important to note that we would expect more stable results from the SII with adolescents 16 years of age and older (Hansen & Campbell, 1985, p. 17). Strong's (1943) early research with the first version of the instrument, the Strong Vocational Interest Blank, found that (a) interests are well-established by 15 years of age (p. 12), (b) interests are remarkably constant from age 15 on (p. 286), and (c) interest scores do not increase with experience in the occupation, that is, occupations are chosen that satisfy interests, not vice versa (p. 51).

According to Super (1973), values, or satisfactions that people seek in life, underlie occupational interests. That is, interests are activities through which values can be expressed. The development of values, too, can be understood from the perspective of social learning theory. That is, they are the products of unique learning experiences, knowledge gained from events and people in the environment, and also from objects, facts, and ideas (Super, 1990).

The Values Scale (VS; Nevill & Super, 1989a) assesses 21 work and nonwork values that people may seek in life. The importance of different values tends to vary with the life stage; for example, adolescents in the Exploration stage may place stronger emphasis on extrinsic values, whereas older adults place greater emphasis on personal values such as Autonomy, Personal Development, and Creativity (Nevill & Super, 1989b). Data from the high school students in the norm group for the VS show that these students most highly valued Achievement, Economic Rewards, and Economic Security. Counselors may use the VS to assess an adolescent's highest and lowest values, guiding him or her to consider how each occupational alternative will satisfy high values and avoid low ones. However, because the VS assesses both work- and nonwork-related values, counselors should encourage adolescents to consider other life roles in which they are currently engaged and in which they will be involved in the future, with a consideration of which values they would like to achieve in each of the relevant life roles.

Super delineates five major life roles that adolescents can be involved in at any particular time: study, work, home/family, leisure, and community service roles. However, some of these roles will be more salient or important to an individual than others at any particular point in time. Many adolescents are holding down at least part-time jobs (in 1992, 41.1% of males aged 16 and 17 and 39.3% of females in this same age group participated in the civilian labor force [U.S. Bureau of the Census, 1993]); and many adolescents are already parents (for every 1,000 females between the ages of 15 and 19, there were 59.9 births in 1990 [U.S. Bureau of the Census, 1993]). Leisure activities also are important to adolescents, especially socializing with peers. The community service role typically does not take on much importance until later in life.

Counselors can use The Salience Inventory (SI; Nevill & Super, 1986c) to assess the relative importance of each of the five life roles: studying, home/family, work, leisure, and community service. The instrument yields Participation (how much time the adolescent spends in role activities), Commitment (to what extent the adolescent emotionally identifies with the role), and Values Expectations (how many values are expected to be expressed in the role in the future) scores for each of the five life roles. The high school sample used for norming the SI demonstrated the highest Participation, Commitment, and Values Expectations scores in leisure and work roles; the lowest were in student and citizen roles. Home and family was the third highest ranked role in the three aspects of salience (Nevill & Super, 1986a, p. 25).

With the information provided by the SI, counselors can help adolescents identify the role(s) in which they currently are spending most of their time, which they are emotionally committed to, and which they expect to be important to them in the future. Counselors can help these adolescents consider how they will prepare for these important future roles and how they will mesh their values with their salient life roles, both in the present and in the future. For example, if an adolescent values Ability Utilization, Altruism, and Prestige, and both work and home/ family roles also are important, the counselor can help the adolescent clarify in which roles he or she hopes to fulfill these values.

The description of the process of career development as basically one of clarifying and implementing the self-concept in the world of work (Super, 1951, 1953 as cited in Herr & Cramer, 1992) has led to the inclusion of self-concept in salient life roles as an important consideration in career counseling. If one's most important life role is home and family, then one's self-concept as a homemaker, spouse, child, and/or parent may be the most crucial variable to consider in counseling. On the other hand, if the work role is the most salient, then how one sees oneself as a worker would be expected to be more important than one's self-concept in the other life roles. The SI can stimulate a discussion of these most important life roles and how one views oneself in each of these arenas.

In Super's view, the salience or importance of the work role is the motivating force behind the development of career maturity. In other words, if an adolescent does not attach much importance to the work role, he or she is unlikely to invest in career planning and exploration, and is therefore unlikely to have acquired much knowledge of the world of work. In turn, this lack of career maturity will hinder the adolescent's ability to cope with the developmental tasks of the Exploration stage of career development: crystallizing ideas about what work is best for him or her, specifying an alternative from those available, and implementing some initial steps toward that alternative. In such cases, stimulation of work salience may be the initial goal of counseling. This can be attempted by helping the adolescent understand that "career" and "work" are interrelated to other life roles, perhaps by completing his or her own Life Career Rainbow (Niles & Usher, 1993).

SUPER'S DEVELOPMENTAL MODEL OF CAREER COUNSELING

An early work by Super (1983) set forth the commonalities and distinctions between the classical, "matching" model of career counseling and the developmental approach. The classical model begins with a preview of assessment data on hand, then moves to more in-depth testing of abilities, interests, and values, proceeds with a review of the data and tentative interpretations, is followed by counseling whereby "matching" of the client's traits with job requirements is facilitated, and ends with follow-up with the client (see Table 3.1). Super (1983) asserts that the flaw in this model is that it assumes that the client is mature enough to have stable traits and to be ready to use the information obtained from the assessment tools. If career maturity is low, then perhaps the counselor should be skeptical about the meaningfulness of the interest and values scores. In these cases, it is questionable if the client would benefit from a review of the aptitude, interest, and values data (Super, 1983).

The primary difference between the classical model and the C-DAC developmental model is that the adolescent's level of career maturity is first ascertained (from the CDI) before confidence is placed in the test results from two of the C-DAC instruments: the VS and the SII. In addition, low work role salience (scores taken from the SI) is examined to provide an explanation for low career maturity scores. If the adolescent does not

TABLE 3.1   A Model of the Classical Career Assessment Process

Step I	Pre-View
	A. Assembly of data on hand
	B. Intake interview
	C. Preliminary assessment
Step II	In-Depth-View: Further Testing?
	A. Level of abilities
	B. Field of interests
	C. Matching and prediction: The individual and occupations
Step III	Assessment of All Data
	A. School and work record
	B. Tests and inventories
	C. Interviews
Step IV	Counseling
	A. Joint review and discussion
	B. Revision or acceptance of assessment and predictions
	C. Discussion of implications for action
	D. Planning action
Step V	Follow-Up
	A. Review of progress
	B. Further planning

Note. From "Assessment in Career Guidance: Toward Truly Developmental Counseling" by D. E. Super, 1983, *The Personnel and Guidance Journal, 61,* pp. 555–562. Copyright 1983 by *The Personnel and Guidance Journal.*

attach much significance to the work role, and has poor planning and exploration attitudes as well as lacks knowledge of the world of work and a particular field of interest, then stimulation of the importance of the work role may be the initial counseling goal set with the adolescent. Low career maturity also may be explained by a belief that one's destiny is not under one's control, lack of autonomy, low self-esteem, low career decision-making self-efficacy (lacking the belief that one can make effective career decisions in the future), and lack of future time orientation, all of which are likely to make career planning and exploration seem remote and irrelevant. These problems, all critical issues to be confronted in the period of adolescence, may have to be initially addressed in counseling before matching of the adolescent's traits with occupational requirements can be attempted.

It is important to keep in mind that the goal of developmental career counseling with adolescents is to help them successfully confront the tasks of the Exploration stage of career development: *crystallizing* their ideas about what work they would be best suited for, *specifying* the most appropriate alternative from those being considered, and *implementing* some initial plans to get started in their chosen career. A broad-based exploration of self and the world of work is necessary first, before more narrowly focused exploration is attempted.

Although college-bound adolescents should be encouraged to explore a variety of career options before making a career decision, there may be more time pressure for non-college-bound students to make an initial decision. In general, however, exploration should be encouraged before commitment to a career takes place. This career exploration should be encouraged through several routes: printed media such as the *Dictionary of Occupational Titles 4th Edition* (U.S. Department of Labor, 1991) and the *Occupational Outlook Handbook 1996–1997 Edition* (U.S. Department of Labor, 1996), audiovisual materials that highlight various occupations, computerized career guidance systems such as DISCOVER and SIGI, information interviews with people currently working in the occupation one is considering, job shadowing (following a worker for a short period of time to learn about a job), volunteer experience, and part-time or summer employment (Yost & Corbishley, 1987).

THREE CASE STUDIES

In the following pages, the C-DAC model is applied to three cases: Carlos, a Hispanic ninth-grade student; Joan, a Caucasian ninth-grader; and Laura, an African American ninth-grader. These C-DAC assessment data were collected from a public high school in Austin, Texas, in October 1992. (For a complete description of the data collection project, see Usher et al., 1994.) However, all of the cases described herein contain some fictional information, inserted to protect the anonymity of the adolescents.

In each of these cases, we begin with Sequence A as suggested by Super et al. (1992) in regards to the interpretation of the inventory results: first the CDI, followed by the SII, the VS, and the SI. Beginning with the CDI places an assessment of career maturity at the forefront of the counseling process. Low career maturity (below the 25th percentile) would suggest that interventions designed to increase career planning attitudes and knowledge of the world of work (such as uncovering reasons for unwillingness to seek out information from certain types of resources, finding alternative sources that are more palatable to the adolescent, and locating acceptable part-time and volunteer job placements) should take priority before the remaining assessments could be expected to have meaning for the client.

The Case of Carlos, a Hispanic, Ninth-Grade Student

Demographic information obtained from Carlos, age 14, revealed that he is the oldest of two children in an intact family. He indicated that his father holds down a 40 hour per week job as an auto mechanic and his mother is not employed outside the home. Carlos aspires to attend a 4-year college or university and dreams of being a professional ball player. He is presently playing baseball on the high school team, but is not currently employed. In the past he has worked for a cable television company. Carlos believes that his father wants him to be a professional ball player, while his mother wants him to have a "good office job." Carlos's grades are "average"; he is not in the gifted program or the vocational program.

Carlos's C-DAC Results

Career Development Inventory:

(Percentile Scores)

Career Planning (CP) 54
Career Exploration (CE) 70
Decision-Making (DM) 02
World-of-Work Information (WW) 25
Career Development Attitudes 59
Career Development Knowledge 07
Career Orientation Total 09

Strong Interest Inventory:

Academic Comfort: 27
Introversion-Extroversion: 68

(continued)

54

Themes:
Realistic .... Mod. Low 44
Investigative .... Mod. Low 41
Artistic .... Mod. Low 40
Enterprising .... Mod. Low 39
Conventional .... Very Low 33
Social .... Very Low 32

Basic Interest Scales:
Average:

Adventure 57
Military Activities 50
Science 49
Music/Drama 48
Writing 42
Athletics 55
Religious Activities 45
Sales 51

Occupations:
Moderately Similar: Bus Driver 42
Farmer 42
Electrician 40
Computer Programmer 42
Restaurant Manager 42
Optician 44

The Values Scale

(Ratings Range from 1 = Low to 4 = High)

3.0 . . . . . Aesthetics
3.0 . . . . . Economic Rewards
3.0 . . . . . Social Interaction
2.8 . . . . . Achievement
2.8 . . . . . Advancement
2.8 . . . . . Creativity
2.8 . . . . . Physical Activity
2.8 . . . . . Cultural Identity
2.6 . . . . . Altruism
2.6 . . . . . Personal Development
2.6 . . . . . Variety
2.4 . . . . . Life Style
2.4 . . . . . Prestige
2.4 . . . . . Working Conditions
2.4 . . . . . Economic Security
2.2 . . . . . Ability Utilization
2.2 . . . . . Risk
2.2 . . . . . Social Relations
2.0 . . . . . Autonomy
1.8 . . . . . Authority
1.4 . . . . . Physical Prowess

(continued)

The Salience Inventory

(Ratings Range from 1 = Low to 4 = High)

	Study	Work	Commmunity Service	Home & Family	Leisure Activities
Participation	2.4	2.6	1.1	3.2	3.3
Commitment	3.1	3.4	1.0	3.3	3.5
Values Expectations	3.5	3.5	1.0	3.6	3.7

Using the C-DAC Battery with Carlos

A review of Carlos's CDI scores sheds light on his readiness to make a career decision. Carlos's CP and CE scores, 54th and 70th percentile, respectively, indicate average to good career planning and exploration attitudes, reflecting that he has given some thought to his career development and has some willingness to engage in career exploration. In particular, the CE score (70th percentile) indicates a good willingness to use a variety of sources of career information and to have found many of these sources helpful in the past. A review of items 31 through 40 on the CDI would indicate what Carlos has actually done to explore his career options. These items ask the respondent to indicate how useful various sources of information have been in the past, such as parents, friends, coaches, teachers, school counselors, books, and other media sources of information. Carlos says that he has gotten a good or great deal of useful information from (a) his father, mother, uncles, and aunts, (b) his school coach, and (c) TV shows, movies, or magazines.

On the other hand, Carlos's career maturity in the knowledge domain is dramatically low. His DM score is at the 2nd percentile, and his WW score is at the 25th percentile. These scores indicate a lack of knowledge of career decision-making principles and knowledge of the world of work. In other words, Carlos knows little about the process by which career decisions are made, and what it takes to get a job and succeed at it. Carlos lacks a broad-based knowledge of the world of work. Therefore, career counseling should first facilitate a broad-based exploration of the world of work before more in-depth exploration of a preferred occupational field is encouraged. With Carlos's relatively high score on willingness to engage in exploration, the counselor could expect him to be a cooperative client in this process.

Given that Carlos knows very little about the world of work, it is questionable whether his SII results are valid. Perhaps his limited knowledge of various occupational titles, school subjects, and activities produced the observed preponderance of "dislike" responses (59% dislikes in occupational category, 75% dislikes in school subjects, and 100% dislikes in activities). This response pattern produced a low-elevated, undifferenti-ated profile: the General Occupational Theme scores ranged from 32 in the Social area to 44 in the Realistic area. None of the Basic Interest Scales were above "average." Carlos did not score "very similar" or "similar" to any occupational group; however, his interest pattern was "moderately similar" to bus driver, farmer, electrician, computer programmer, restau-rant manager, and optician. The Introversion-Extroversion score (68) indi-cated a preference for working with things or ideas, and his Academic Comfort score was low (27), perhaps indicating a preference for pursuing practical subjects and occupations rather than theoretical or philosophi-cal ones.

Although "professional athlete" is not one of the occupational groups to which a client's pattern of interests can be compared on the SII, it is noteworthy that Carlos scored "moderately dissimilar" to athletic trainer. His score on the Athletics Basic Interest was only "average." It might be fruitful to pursue with Carlos what attracts him to the professional athlete career and what differences he displays from athletic trainers. Perhaps professional athletics is one avenue that Hispanic group members see as a viable alternative to participating in the dominant group's educational system (see Ogbu, 1990, for a discussion of cultural models), although Carlos does aspire to go to college. Although Carlos's grades would allow him to apply to colleges of medium selectivity, the counselor might explore his expectations about achieving college entrance. If he aspires to college but does not expect to achieve entrance (a common problem for minority group members), then the counselor should explore what he perceives the barriers to be and how those barriers might be overcome.

Because Carlos plays baseball on the school team, perhaps he has selected this career direction based on this one skill he has exhibited. Due to his limited knowledge of the world of work as indicated by the CDI, he may not be aware of the myriad of career options available to him. Limited exposure to occupational role models and restricted access to career opportunities have historically been barriers to minority group members' career development. This could explain Carlos's myopic expres-sion of inventoried interests and lack of career vision. Furthermore, Car-los's family's influence on his career decision, especially in light of his belief that his father wants him to be a professional ball player and the strong identification with the family in Hispanic culture, should be explored.

An additional concern in counseling Carlos would be that as students adhere to the professional athlete dream, with all its promise of glory and riches, they become entrenched in a system that segregates them from nonathletes, and continues to focus their attention on athletic partici-pation and a sport career (Wooten & Hinkle, 1994). The reality, however, is that only about 3.3% of college athletes continue in a professional sport career (Remer et al., 1978, as cited in Wooten & Hinkle, 1994); thus, it is imperative that student athletes develop career alternatives. Furthermore, if Carlos has focused on his abilities in this one area, sport, counseling should facilitate self-exploration as much as career exploration. What other activities does Carlos enjoy, and what additional skills and abilities does Carlos have? What does Carlos want out of life? The VS and SI results can shed light on this last question.

Carlos's highest and lowest values from the VS provide some data to develop hypotheses about what he hopes to achieve through his expressed dream of a professional sport career, as well as in other life roles. His four highest values are Economic Rewards (having a high standard of living), Social Interaction (doing things with other people), Aesthetics (making life more beautiful), and Creativity (discovering, developing, or designing new things). It would be productive to explore with Carlos in what roles he sees his aesthetics and creativity values being fulfilled. We could speculate that economic rewards and social interaction could be achieved in a professional sport career. Carlos's three lowest values, those he would want to avoid, are Physical Prowess (working hard physically), Authority (telling others what to do), and Autonomy (acting on one's own). How does he see a professional athlete avoiding working hard physically? Perhaps Carlos equated the items on this scale with menial labor tasks that require physical exertion. The low value on authority and autonomy perhaps reflects a team spirit or perspective inculcated by team sport participation. However, the lack of importance attached to authority might prevent Carlos from pursuing a leadership role in athletics.

Overall, Carlos's inventoried values show an importance attached to monetary rewards with less concern about economic security, authority, and autonomy, all of which seems consistent with a professional athletic career. However, his desire to avoid physical exertion should be explored in counseling, as well as the value attached to creativity and aesthetics. How does Carlos hope to achieve these values in his life? Could he explore other occupations that might provide fulfillment of these values, in addition to his other expectations?

The SI scores indicate what life roles are most important to Carlos now and those he expects to be most important in the future. The community service role appears irrelevant to Carlos now, and he does not expect to fulfill many of his values in that role in the future. The remaining four life roles appear to have equal and major significance to Carlos for the future. Perhaps Carlos is unsure in which future roles he will be able to achieve most of his values. Studying and working are of equal future importance to Carlos, again confirming that the student role holds promise for him in the future. The work role also is important to Carlos, providing good motivation for the development of career maturity. Work is significant for him, and he is therefore more likely to think ahead and plan for his future in work as well as assimilate information about the world of work as he experiences it, perhaps through part-time jobs. Because the four life roles appear to be of equal importance to Carlos in the future, the question remains, "Which values does he want to achieve in which life roles?" This question can be answered by referring back to the items on the Values Expectation scale of the SI. On this scale, respondents are asked to rate the degree to which they see the opportunity to achieve each value in the various five life roles. For example, Carlos responded that he sees the opportunity to "make life more beautiful" (i.e., value on Aesthetics) to a great extent in the home/family role, and to little or no extent in the working role. Fourteen of the 21 values from the VS are covered in this manner.

Carlos's current participation scores reveal that he spends more time in his home/family life and leisure activities than in his studying and working activities; however, he seems emotionally committed to all roles except community service. He seems fairly balanced in his role salience, yet counseling might include a consideration of how Carlos's time investments in home/family and leisure activities affect his grades in school and how this might influence his ability to achieve academically in the future. However, the importance of his home/family life (evident from his high participation, commitment, and future expectations scores) should be honored by the counselor, because much value is placed on home and family in Hispanic culture.

The Case of Joan, a Caucasian Ninth-Grade Student

Joan, age 15 at the time of the C-DAC battery administration, indicated that she is the younger of two children in an intact family. Her father has been employed for 16 years as a physician, and her mother is not employed outside of the home. Joan aspires to attend a 4-year college or university and was able to list three occupational interests in the following order of preference: architect, psychologist, and interior designer. Joan is not currently working but indicated that she has sporadically worked in her father's medical office as a clerk. She participates in two school sports and is enrolled in several honors classes. Joan's grades are above average in all subjects. Joan believes that her mother would like her to become an interior designer or architect, while her father wants her to "do whatever I want to do."

Joan's C-DAC Results

Career Development Inventory

(Percentile Scores)

Career Planning 77
Career Exploration 97
Decision-Making 60
World-of-Work Information 95
Career Development Attitudes 90
Career Development Knowledge 88
Career Orientation Total 90

Strong Interest Inventory

Academic Comfort 57
Introversion-Extroversion 35

Themes:
Artistic .... Very High 65
Social .... Average 54
Investigative .... Average 54
Realistic .... Average 45
Enterprising .... Mod. Low 42
Conventional .... Very Low 33

Basic Interest Scales:
Very High: Art 67
                  Adventure 65
High: Music/Drama 65
                  Nature 62
Moderately High: Writing 59
                  Teaching 56
                  Social Service 60
                  Athletics 55
                  Domestic Arts 60
                  Medical Science 57
                  Agriculture 56

Occupations:
Very Similar: Commercial Artist 58
                  Photographer 57
                  Musician 59
                  Chef 59
                  Broadcaster 55
Similar: Fine Artist 47
                  Flight Attendant 54

(continued)

	Advertising Executive	48
	Nurse, RN	47
	Recreation Leader	47
Moderately Similar:	Medical Illustrator	44
	Art Teacher	43
	Reporter	44
	Occupational Therapist	42
	Speech Pathologist	44
	YWCA Director	41
	Physical Therapist	43
	Police Officer	41

The Values Scale

(Ratings Range from 1 = Low to 4 = High)

4.0 ..... Ability Utilization
4.0 ..... Achievement
4.0 ..... Advancement
4.0 ..... Aesthetics
4.0 ..... Personal Development
3.8 ..... Altruism
3.8 ..... Creativity
3.8 ..... Life Style
3.6 ..... Autonomy
3.6 ..... Economic Rewards
3.6 ..... Social Relations
3.6 ..... Economic Security
3.4 ..... Prestige
3.2 ..... Physical Activity
3.2 ..... Risk
3.2 ..... Social Interaction
3.2 ..... Variety
3.2 ..... Working Conditions
3.0 ..... Authority
3.0 ..... Cultural Identity
1.8 ..... Physical Prowess

The Salience Inventory

(Ratings Range from 1 = Low to 4 = High)

	Study	Work	Community Service	Home & Family	Leisure Activities
Participation	3.1	1.3	2.0	3.0	3.8
Commitment	3.5	3.1	3.0	3.7	3.9
Values Expectations	3.7	3.7	2.7	3.5	3.6

Using the C-DAC Battery with Joan

First, examining Joan's CDI scores, her attitudinal scores on career maturity are well above average (77th percentile for career planning and 97th percentile for career exploration). These scores indicate that Joan has given a considerable amount of attention, thought, and planning to her career development and is willing to use a variety of sources of information to help her make career decisions. Her scores also indicate that she has already found many kinds of information useful to her in the career-planning process. The counselor could review with Joan what sources she has actually used and reinforce her behavior in this exploration process. Exploration with additional sources of information should be encouraged, because Joan would be a willing explorer.

Joan's high cognitive scores on the CDI are puzzling given the lack of work experience indicated on her demographic sheet. How has she managed to acquire such a large amount of knowledge about the world of work (95th percentile)? Obviously, she has learned much from her exploratory activities and inquiring attitude, perhaps through contact with workers in a variety of occupations at her father's medical office. Her DM score at the 60th percentile, while above average, could indicate an area of development for Joan; the counselor could help her develop a more thorough understanding of how effective career decisions are made. That is, while Joan may know much, she may need help in applying that knowledge to her own career planning. Additionally, the counselor could encourage Joan to get work experience in the preferred area to help her with the exploration task of specification.

With such high career maturity scores indicated by the CDI, more confidence can be placed in Joan's interest inventory results from the SII. Joan's profile is differentiated, with the General Occupational Theme scores ranging from a low of 33 in the Conventional area to a high of 65 in the Artistic area. Across all parts of the inventory, Joan said she "liked" 45% of the items and "disliked" 31% of them. She was "indifferent" to 24% of the items. Clearly, Joan is able to distinguish among occupations, school subjects, activities, leisure activities, and types of people that she likes and does not like.

Joan's interests seem to lie in the direction of artistic pursuits; she scored "very high" on the Artistic area followed by General Occupational Theme scores that were only "average" or below. Within the Artistic area, she scored high on all of the Basic Interest Scales: Music/Drama, Art, and Writing. Her pattern of responses on the SII was similar to several occupational groups within the Artistic area. For example, her profile was very similar to satisfied commercial artists, photographers, musicians, chefs, and broadcasters. The counselor should explore with Joan whether these occupations hold any appeal for her. In addition, a list of other occupations with similar characteristics should be generated for exploratory purposes.

It is interesting to note that Joan's SII results only indicate "midrange similarity" to psychologist and interior decorator, two of her occupational choices. Joan's interests are "moderately dissimilar" to architect, her first choice occupation. For females, architect is a primarily Realistic occupation, and Joan only scored "average" in this area. Psychologist is a primarily Investigative occupation, and interior decorator contains elements of Enterprising. Joan only has "average" interest in the Investigative area, and "moderately low" interest in the Enterprising area. The counselor should facilitate a discussion of what characteristics Joan has in common with people in these occupations and those that make her "different from" them as well.

Although Joan is on the right track in considering a variety of Artistic careers, perhaps she would find more satisfaction in those that were more purely "artistic." This interpretation is supported by her high academic comfort score, which implies an interest in theoretical, philosophical pursuits as opposed to practical applications of knowledge. One might guess that Joan is being encouraged by her parents to choose an artistic career "in which she can make a living." Although this is certainly an important consideration in making a career choice, the counselor should facilitate Joan's exploration of the job openings in the more purely artistic areas before Joan closes them off as possibilities.

In addition, because Joan's scores indicate (a) a preference for working with people (low introversion-extroversion score), (b) moderately high interest on most of the Social Basic Interest Scales, and (c) similarity to nurses and recreation leaders, Joan should be encouraged to explore social occupations that have artistic elements. Nevertheless, from her SII results, one would still expect Joan to be most satisfied in a primarily artistic occupation. The question remains, however, "How much will Joan's interests change in the next several years?"

Although interests are one of the primary determinants of career satisfaction, other factors also need to be considered. Does Joan want to express her artistic interests in work? What artistic abilities and skills does she have? How does she currently display them? What skills does she want to develop? Does Joan have the self-confidence and self-efficacy in regards to her artistic abilities that will allow her to use them in a work setting? If not, the counselor might help her strengthen her self-image in this area.

Joan's values also need to be considered in her career planning. However, her VS results do not provide much distinction among the values assessed. The scores do indicate that she wants to avoid Physical

Prowess (working hard physically). The scores on the remainder of the values, however, range from 3.0 to 4.0. That is, at this point in time, Joan considers all of these values important to her. Most important are Aesthetics, Ability Utilization, Achievement, Advancement, and Personal Development. Creativity was rated 3.8. Economic and social concerns are also rated important to Joan. With this type of VS profile, the counselor needs to provide additional structure to help Joan sort out what is most important to her. For example, Joan could be asked to write down her 10 most important values, and then to cross them off one at a time, until only one remains. If Joan can be helped to identify her high and low values, then career choices can be examined for their likelihood to fulfill her high values and avoid her low ones. Furthermore, in Joan's case, a possible discrepancy between value placed on social interaction with others and interest in artistic careers that may not provide that kind of people contact should be seriously examined.

The SI can provide some clues as to how Joan might want to express her interests and meet her values. Currently, she is not participating in work to any extent, and she spends most of her time in leisure activities (this may include the time she spends participating in two school sports). Her studies and family activities consume about an equal amount of Joan's time.

In terms of Joan's emotional identification with various roles, work appears more important but still lags behind leisure, home and family, and the student role. However, she expects work to become even more salient in the future, along with her studies, leisure activities, and home/ family life. This profile shows a girl who expects the student and worker role to become even more significant in her life, but who also wants to maintain a commitment to leisure and her home and family roles. Although Joan's indication of involvement in the community service role is lower than that of the other life roles, she still expects it to fulfill some of her values.

It appears that Joan expects to be involved in all of the life roles to some extent. Although this expectation coincides well with her future plans of going to college, Joan could possibly benefit from counseling that addresses how she expects to achieve this role balance. In terms of career planning, the counselor should help Joan clarify in which roles she expects to achieve which values and express which interests. Again, her responses to the Values Expectation scale items from the SI should be examined. For example, does she expect her value on Aesthetics to be met in the worker role, and does she expect her Artistic interests to be expressed in her work? In what roles does she expect her Social interests and values on Social Relations and Social Interaction to be met? To help

Joan clarify her life role activities, counseling should facilitate the trial expression of Joan's interests and values within a variety of roles.

The Case of Laura, an African American Ninth-Grade Student

Although in the ninth grade, Laura indicated that she was 17 years of age at the time of the C-DAC test administration. One can assume from this that she has been retained in lower grades for several years and therefore is most likely academically underprepared. Laura does not participate in any extracurricular school activities; she works approximately 25 hours per week as a cashier at a local supermarket. Laura aspires to attend a 2-year college or community college and indicated three occupational interests in the following order: secretary, lawyer, and beautician. Laura is the youngest of five children in an intact family. Her father works part-time as a mechanic and her mother is a caregiver for children in her home on a full-time basis. Laura believes that her parents want her to have a "good" job but have not encouraged any particular occupations.

Laura's C-DAC Results

Career Development Inventory

(Percentile Scores)

Career Planning	48
Career Exploration	92
Decision-Making	01
World-of-Work Information	07
Career Development Attitudes	70
Career Development Knowledge	01
Career Orientation Total	32

Strong Interest Inventory

Academic Comfort	22
Introversion-Extroversion	51

Themes:

Conventional	Mod. High	57
Enterprising	Mod. High	55
Artistic	Average	49
Social	Average	49
Investigative	Low	36
Realistic	Low	36

Basic Interest Scales:

Very High:	Sales	66
High:	Office Practices	64
	Athletics	58

(continued)

Occupations:

Similar:	Banker	50
	Nursing Home Administrator	45
	Food Service Manager	47
	Secretary	46
	Air Force Enlisted Personnel	50
	Marine Corps Enlisted	46
	Chamber of Commerce Executive	53
	Funeral Director	49
	Optician	50
	Beautician	48
	Buyer	52
Moderately Similar:	Credit Manager	40
	Executive Housekeeper	44
	Dental Assistant	40
	Army Enlisted Personnel	43
	Store Manager	41
	Florist	43
	Physical Therapist	43
	Advertising Executive	41
	Elementary Teacher	42
	Navy Enlisted Personnel	43

The Values Scale

(Ratings Range from 1 = Low to 4 = High)

3.8 . . . . . Autonomy
3.6 . . . . . Life Style
3.4 . . . . . Altruism
3.4 . . . . . Creativity
3.4 . . . . . Personal Development
3.4 . . . . . Economic Security
3.2 . . . . . Achievement
3.2 . . . . . Economic Rewards
3.0 . . . . . Ability Utilization
3.0 . . . . . Aesthetics
3.0 . . . . . Prestige
3.0 . . . . . Physical Prowess
2.8 . . . . . Advancement
2.8 . . . . . Working Conditions
2.8 . . . . . Cultural Identity
2.6 . . . . . Physical Activity
2.6 . . . . . Risk
2.6 . . . . . Social Interaction
2.6 . . . . . Social Relations
2.4 . . . . . Authority
2.2 . . . . . Variety

(continued)

The Salience Inventory

(Ratings Range from 1 = Low to 4 = High)

	Study	Work	Community Service	Home & Family	Leisure Activities
Participation	2.4	3.1	2.4	2.4	1.0
Commitment	2.0	3.8	2.4	3.3	1.0
Values Expectations	1.8	3.8	3.0	3.8	1.0

Using the C-DAC Battery with Laura

Laura's CDI scores indicate a moderate amount of thought and planning given to her career development (48th percentile on CP) but high willingness to engage in career planning activities (92nd percentile on CE) compared with other ninth graders. Her low cognitive scores on DM and WW indicate an extreme lack of knowledge about how to make effective career decisions and how to find and succeed at a job. In other words, Laura is willing to explore, but has only done a moderate amount of it. She has acquired very little information about the world of work in general. Laura lacks a broad-based knowledge of careers. Therefore, the counselor should begin with broad-based exploration activities (for example, helping Laura understand a system by which the world of work is organized) before encouraging Laura to explore careers with more specificity. Laura has time to do this needed exploration, if she remains in school for the three additional years she needs to graduate.

Because Laura's career maturity scores are so low, the counselor should question the validity of her SII results. The counselor should wonder whether Laura has enough knowledge and experience to know whether she likes or dislikes certain occupations, activities, types of people, and so forth.

However, some of Laura's SII scores are consistent with her work experience and occupational choices. Her Holland code is CEA(S), with the Conventional and Enterprising scores being virtually the same (moderately high), as well as the Artistic and Social scores (average). Laura's Realistic and Investigative theme scores are both identical and low. Her Basic Interest Scale scores indicate high interest in athletics, office practices, and sales. Although Laura did not score "very similar" to any of the occupational groups, she shows similarity of interest patterns to secretary and beautician, two of her occupational choices. That is, according to Holland's theory, Laura is likely to be reinforced for her personality characteristics in these two occupations, thus leading to job satisfaction. Laura's counselor should encourage more in-depth exploration of these two occupations, in addition to the other occupations suggested by her profile. Laura should then be encouraged to develop a more extensive list of occupations to explore that are similar to the suggested ones and that hold appeal for her.

Laura's scores indicate that she is "very dissimilar" to her third occupational choice, lawyer. This would appear to be an unrealistic career choice for Laura, given her poor school grades as well as her low academic comfort score. Her Academic Comfort score indicates an interest in applied subjects and an avoidance of research and theoretical pursuits. The legal profession requires extensive investigative activities that Laura likely would find unrewarding. It would be informative to discover why Laura fantasizes about this occupation, which would provide clues as to what she seeks in work. For example, does she dream about it because it is one of the highest paid professions? Does she seek economic rewards in her own career? How much money does Laura aspire to make in her job when she leaves school? How willing is Laura to defer making money in order to attend college? These questions should be raised by Laura's counselor.

Laura's scores on the VS can provide some information as to what she might want to get out of the work role. However, her scores on the 21 values range from 2.2 to 3.8; all are above average. Like Joan, Laura needs some help from her counselor in specifying low versus high values. Perhaps Laura could be asked to sort these 21 values into three piles: "those that I can't live without," "those that I definitely don't want," and "those that I'd like to have but don't need."

According to the VS scores, Laura's highest value is Autonomy; her lowest is Variety. She does seem to place importance on Economic Rewards (3.2) and Economic Security (3.4) but she also seeks Life Style (3.6), Altruism (3.4), Creativity (3.4), Personal Development (3.4), and Achievement (3.2). Laura's counselor needs to explore with her in which life roles Laura hopes to achieve these values. Which ones does she want to fulfill in the work role? The occupations she is considering can then be examined for their likelihood of meeting her high values and avoiding her low ones. For example, the occupation of Beautician is likely to provide for more autonomy and creativity than Secretary, yet secretarial positions may provide more stable income. Each occupational alternative should be examined for its ability to fulfill Laura's high values and avoid her low ones.

Laura's high value on Altruism prompts the question, "In which life role(s) does Laura want to help make the world a better place or help people lead better lives in some way?" The SI results provide a picture of which roles are most important to Laura. In terms of time spent in a role, Laura participates to the greatest extent in work. About an equal amount of her time is then devoted to her studies, her community service activities (perhaps church activities), and her home and family life. She reports little time spent in leisure activities.

Laura's Commitment scores indicate that she emotionally identifies to the greatest extent with work, followed by home and family, community service, studying, and leisure, in that order. Again, her work salience appears high, and she shows obvious commitment to home and family and to community service. The student and leisure roles are less emotionally salient for Laura.

Laura's pattern of future importance attached to each role is similar. Laura expects more of her values to be met in the work and family roles in the future, followed by community service. The study role drops slightly in importance for Laura and her future expectations for the leisure role remain the same. Overall, Laura has high work salience, in the present and for the future, which is a good indication that she will view career planning in the present as important to her future work status. However, her lower Values Expectation score for the student role may be problematic if she plans to attend college after high school graduation. This will be a crucial area for counseling as Laura proceeds through the career planning process.

Because family and community service also are extremely important to Laura, her counselor should explore which values she expects to meet in each of them. One hypothesis would be that Laura expects her Altruistic values to be met in the family and/or community service roles, rather than in work, especially in light of her SII results, which indicate little interest in the Social (helping others) theme. Counseling should facilitate Laura's consideration of which values she will attempt to meet in each of her salient roles: work, family, and community service.

In addition, to achieve a more balanced approach to life, the counselor could help Laura consider how she might incorporate leisure into her lifestyle, especially in light of her interest in Athletics (from the SII) and her value on Physical Prowess (3.0). However, the counselor needs to be sensitive to economic limitations for certain leisure activities that many members of minority groups face.

SUMMARY

Adolescents typically are in the Exploration stage of Super's career development model, and the C-DAC model can successfully be used to facilitate their career decision making, as was demonstrated in three case studies.

The next chapter examines the use of this model with college students.

4

Career Counseling With College Students

This chapter deals with the career development stage of college students, how the career development theory of Donald E. Super applies to them, and how career counseling can be used with college students, and provides three case studies demonstrating the use of the Career Development, Assessment, and Counseling (C-DAC) approach with them.

THE DEVELOPMENTAL STAGE

Most undergraduate students enter their collegiate experience working on tasks related to Super's (1957) Exploratory stage (see Figure 1.1). Individuals begin this stage with an awareness that an occupation will be part of life. Super divided the Exploratory stage into three phases: fantasy, tentative, and realistic.

In the fantasy phase, which is very common for entering freshmen, the preferred occupational options tend to be unrealistic, reflecting little understanding of self. Preferred options may change easily and frequently, due to this low self-awareness and an inadequate knowledge of the world of work. The individuals in this phase approach the world of work as if they could do anything, often neglecting the reality that their options may be limited by supply and demand, and that competition for employment may require compromise.

As an individual enters into the second phase of the Exploratory stage, the tentative phase, his or her self-awareness and knowledge of the world of work have increased to the point where only a limited number of occupational alternatives are being explored. Considerable uncertainty remains during this phase concerning individual abilities, values, and interests, on one hand, and training requirements and occupational opportunities on the other. In many cases, college students are forced into the tentative phase because of the need to choose a major by the end of their sophomore year or, in some cases, even sooner. Completing the necessary tasks of any stage or phase cannot be realistically forced because working through specific tasks is based on the individual's own maturity and development. Therefore, it is common for students to choose majors that are inappropriate. Subsequently, many college students change majors several times, and some students are not happy with their occupational options upon graduation.

As students enter the realistic phase of the Exploratory stage, they narrow their list of occupational alternatives and the related majors that will prepare them for their occupational choices. This phase completes the Exploratory stage, ending for most individuals in their mid-20s, and results in less than satisfying career development for some. It is not surprising to find individuals who are unhappy with their choices even after 4 years of college, because many college students make occupational choices before reaching a level of maturity needed for developmental tasks typical of the mid-20s. The career counseling process can assist individuals in making satisfying occupational choices, but it is not possible to force an individual to mature before they are ready. Educational systems that are rigid about age and grade matching are inconsistent with the natural development of many individuals. In college there is somewhat greater acceptance of students discontinuing their educational pursuits to gain life experience to facilitate the maturation process than in some other situations.

SUPER'S THEORY AS IT APPLIES TO COLLEGE STUDENTS

Super's career development theory provides a useful way of understanding college students and a basis for conducting career counseling with them.

Gelso and Fretz (1992) have described Super's theory as a "Developmental Self-Concept Approach," and Super (1969) states that his theory of career development is based on differential-developmental-social-phenomenological psychology. He suggests, as do Crites (1969) and Borow (1982), that his theory is not integrated or comprehensive, but rather "a loosely unified set of theories dealing with specific aspects of career development, taken from developmental, differential, social, personality, and phenomenological psychology and held together by self-concept and learning theory." Super (1990) believes that each segment of his theory provides testable hypotheses, and that the tested and refined segments will eventually lead to an integrated theory.

The use of intelligence and aptitude tests by the military are the elements that Super took from differential psychology. From developmental psychology, he sought to explain how individual abilities and interests affect behavior. His consideration of occupational mobility and environmental influences on career choice were derived from sociology, and the work of Rogers (1951) on self-concept and personal construct theories is a significant contributor to his observation of personality theory and how it affects people and their decision making. Super's current "segmental theory" resulted from the integration of these various theoretical perspectives.

Although Super (1969) states that his theory is not comprehensive, it provides a multifaceted view of many factors that influence an individual in the process of career development and decision making. This broad, multifaceted view provides a dynamic model on which to base career services for college students.

Super also has developed assessment instruments that facilitate the identification of an individual's career maturity, interests, values, and work roles. These instruments are very helpful in providing a significant amount of information to a student concerning the many factors relevant to career choice in a limited amount of time and, because of the credibility that students often attribute to "tests," help to reduce the resistance that many of them have to career counseling.

Super (1953) originally composed 10 propositions that are relevant to the career development process. Later, Super (1990) expanded these propositions to be inclusive of more recent career development research (Fisher, 1989; Gribbons & Lohnes, 1968, 1982; Jordaan & Heyde, 1979; Kleinberg, 1976; Super & Bachrach, 1957; Super, Kowalski, & Gotkin, 1967; Super & Overstreet, 1960). The resulting 14 propositions provide a strong conceptual framework for career services, as shown in Table 4.1. They take into account an individual's abilities, personality characteristics, interests, traits, self-concepts, aptitudes, physical makeup, the opportunities that an individual has to observe and act out various life roles, and the effect that approval or disapproval of this role playing by superiors and peers has on the individual, family history, socioeconomic level, mental ability, education, skills, racial and ethnic biases, opportunities, and social traditions.

One might say that this is a rather comprehensive assessment or view of an individual, a view that is artistically illustrated in Super's (1990) Archway Model (see Figure 1.2). Few individuals who are attending college have ever had the opportunity to look at themselves in a way that thoroughly addresses this composite of factors. Such a comprehensive view of an individual facilitates the career decision-making process through enhancing the individual's ability to match oneself with compatible occupations and academic majors that lead to them. Conversely, the failure to adequately identify the factors that make up self-concept and

TABLE 4.1 Super's Fourteen Propositions Relevant to Career Development

1. People differ in their abilities and personalities, needs, values, interests, traits, and self-concepts.
2. People are qualified, by virtue of these characteristics, each for a number of occupations.
3. Each occupation requires a characteristic pattern of abilities and personality traits, with tolerances wide enough to allow both some variety of occupations for each individual and some variety of individuals in each occupation.
4. Vocational preferences and competencies, the situations in which people live and work, and, hence, their self-concepts change with time and experience, although self-concepts, as products of social learning, are increasingly stable from late adolescence until late maturity, providing some continuity in choice and adjustment.
5. This process of change may be summed up in a series of life stages (a "maxicycle") characterized as a sequence of growth, exploration, establishment, maintenance, and decline, and these stages may in turn be subdivided into (a) the fantasy, tentative, and realistic phases of the exploratory stage and (b) the trial and stable phases of the establishment stage. A small (mini) cycle takes place in transitions from one stage to the next or each time an individual is destabilized by a reduction in force, changes in type of manpower needs, illness or injury, or other socioeconomic or personal events. Such unstable or multiple-trial careers involve new growth, reexploration, and reestablishment (recycling).
6. The nature of the career pattern—that is, the occupational level attained and the sequence, frequency, and duration of trial and stable jobs—is determined by the individual's parental socioeconomic level, mental ability, education, skills, personality characteristics (needs, values, interests, traits, and self-concepts), and career maturity and by the opportunities to which he or she is exposed.
7. Success in coping with the demands of the environment and of the organism in that context at any given life-career stage depends on the readiness of the individual to cope with these demands (that is, on his or her career maturity). Career maturity is a constellation of physical, psychological, and social characteristics; psychologically, it is both cognitive and affective. It includes the degree of success in coping with the demands of earlier stages and substages of career development, and especially with the most recent.
8. Career maturity is a hypothetical construct. Its operational definition is perhaps as difficult to formulate as is that of intelligence, but its history is much briefer and its achievements even less definitive.

TABLE 4.1 Continued

Contrary to the impressions created by some writers, it does not increase monotonically, and it is not a unitary trait.

 9. Development through the life stages can be guided, partly by facilitating the maturing of abilities and interests and partly by aiding in reality testing and in the development of self-concepts.
10. The process of career development is essentially that of developing and implementing occupational self-concepts. It is a synthesizing and compromising process in which the self-concept is a product of the interaction of inherited aptitudes, physical makeup, opportunity to observe and play various roles, and evaluations of the extent to which the results of role playing meet with the approval of superiors and fellows (interactive learning).
11. The process of synthesis of or compromise between individual and social factors, between self-concepts and reality, is one of role playing and of learning from feedback, whether the role is played fantasy, in the counseling interview, or in such real-life activities as classes, clubs, part-time work, and entry jobs.
12. Work satisfactions and life satisfactions depend on the extent to which the individual finds adequate outlets for abilities, needs, values, interests, personality traits, and self-concepts. They depend on establishment in a type of work, a work situation, and a way of life in which one can play the kind of role that growth and exploratory experiences have led one to consider congenial and appropriate.
13. The degree of satisfaction people attain from work is proportional to the degree to which they have been able to implement self-concepts.
14. Work and occupation provide a focus for personality organization for most men and women, although for some persons this focus is peripheral, incidental, or even nonexistent. Then other foci, such as leisure activities and homemaking, may be central. (Social traditions, such as sex-role stereotyping and modeling, racial and ethnic biases, and the opportunity structure, as well as individual differences, are important determinants of preferences for such roles as worker, student, leisurite, homemaker, and citizen.)

other elements of self can lead to decisions about careers and academic majors that are misleading and costly to the individual in the attainment of personally meaningful goals.

The years for the traditional college student, ages 18 to 23, are also a time when the process of individuation is naturally occurring, and therefore learning about oneself is especially important. Too often students choose majors that are based on what is popular with friends or suggested by parents, relying on individuals who have inadequate knowledge of the world of work and who lack objectivity (Ginzberg, 1971).

Flanagan (1973) reported that after 6 years only 13% of his sample of boys reported the same occupational choice they had identified in the 11th grade. Weissberg, Berentsen, Cote, Cravey, and Heath (1982) found that 80% of the college students surveyed indicated a moderate or strong need related to career development, and 72% indicated a moderate or strong need to explore their interests, values, and abilities as they related to educational/career alternatives. These findings support the conclusion that many college students have had inadequate counseling to facilitate their understanding of self and too little exposure to information concerning their occupational alternatives, two primary elements involved in career decision making.

The developmental nature of career counseling is strongly supported by Super (1954). In his theory, the developmental process that relates to different tasks for the various stages of life is combined with the trait and factor approach, such as Williamson's (1950) and Holland's (1973, 1974) modified trait and factor theory.

The developmental nature of Super's theory is illustrated in his Life-Career Rainbow (Super, 1980) (see Figure 1.3). The Life-Career Rainbow provides a model of the stages of career development, as defined by Super, and their correlation to life roles. Different roles relate to different tasks of career development, as defined by various developmental stages.

A concept related to career development is that of career maturity. An individual's career maturity (Crites, 1973; Super, 1955, 1974) relates to one's life span and is defined as the individual's readiness to cope with the developmental tasks found during a particular stage of development. The age at which one is expected to accomplish specific stage-related tasks is defined by society. For college students, as has previously been indicated, the expected stage of career development is generally considered to be Exploration, although the entry into the Establishment stage begins for some as they approach graduation and participate in cooperative education experiences or internships.

The career development process is lifelong, and therefore through counseling one can be guided as one's self-concept matures and changes. The process can be orderly with minimal cost to the individual if careful evaluation is done at each stage regarding what steps to follow that will best promote one's identified career path. "Recycling" is the nature of the process as the individual matures, or develops, in their understanding of self and their place in the world of work.

In other words, the individual may return to the Exploratory stage whenever it is appropriate to do so, generally based on changes within or external to the individual. The concept of matching self with occupation is clear and perhaps best described as a "synthesizing and compromising process." This process includes both cognitive and affective elements of self that are compared to occupational alternatives, and is a process that can best be facilitated by counselors and psychologists who have received specific training in career counseling.

The fact that most colleges and universities provide career counseling for students at little or no charge clearly reflects the value it has for individuals in making educational and occupational decisions. In addition, educating students as to what is involved in the career decision-making process provides them with skills and information that can readily be generalized to virtually every personal decision they make in life. Understanding one's self is an essential component of any personal decision and also facilitates the process of individuation.

As a result of an extensive literature review, Brown and Lent (1984) have identified 10 major developmental themes related to career counseling (Table 4.2). The identified themes are intended to approximate the content domain of vocational development theory from 1967 to 1981.

TABLE 4.2 Brown and Lent's Vocational Development Themes

1. Vocational Choice Expression—expressed concepts of self-in-future occupation
2. Vocational Choice Realism—comparison between characteristics of the chosen occupation and societal requirements and expectations for members of that occupation
3. Vocational Choice Rationale—expressed reasons or criteria for choosing occupations
4. Vocational Choice Attitudes—inventoried thoughts and feelings about the process of choosing an occupation
5. Vocational Decision-Making Processes—organizing and deliberating about information regarding actions construed as means for entering occupations
6. Work Values—affect toward concepts of anticipated occupational outcomes
7. Job Satisfaction—affect toward concepts of past job experiences
8. Occupational Knowledge—factual information about occupations in general and the labor/occupational structure
9. Vocational Exploratory Behavior—activity undertaken to elicit information about self-in-occupations
10. Job Adjustment—comparison between person's performance in a job and the general job role expectations for that setting

Note. From *Handbook of Counseling Psychology* by S.D. Brown and R.W. Lent, 1991, John Wiley & Sons, New York. Reprinted by permission.

It is apparent that Super's developmental theory fits within their scope and may have strongly influenced these themes. Through an oblique analysis of their longitudinal study of 9th and 12th grade boys, Jordaan and Heyde (1979) identified factors that were quite similar to those in the 10 themes in Table 4.2.

THE C-DAC MODEL EXPLAINED

The C-DAC model is the application of innovative assessment and counseling, in conjunction with developmental theory, for the purpose of career decision making. The C-DAC model represents the blend of counseling strategies with state-of-the-art career assessment. Crites (1974) has identified the advantages of including psychological testing. These advantages are:

1. Counselors can be taught to use tests more easily than they can be trained to use other methods of observation, such as rating scales or interviews.
2. Tests are subject to less bias than other methods of observation. That is not to say that tests cannot be influenced by the prejudices or beliefs of the test constructors, but with tests the biases can be controlled to a greater extent.
3. Observations made through tests are more easily communicated than observations made through other means.
4. Tests reduce the time necessary for information gathering; in other words, they provide a shortcut to the information.
5. Tests provide a standard of comparison against which a person can judge herself or himself and thus improve self-evaluation.
6. Tests provide people with a sample of their psychological traits to use in developing hypotheses about themselves.

A COUNSELING APPROACH ILLUSTRATING THE C-DAC MODEL

When working with college students who have had little or no previous career counseling, it is often best to start with a model that is simple but consistent with Super's (1990) 14 propositions. Subsequently, a basic model of the career counseling process, one that has been effectively utilized with university students, is provided in Table 4.3.

As noted in Table 4.3, there are two fundamental elements involved in making a major or career decision. The first involves having a good understanding of one's self or identity, and the second is related to being aware of curriculum/occupational options in the world of work.

TABLE 4.3 A Career Decision-Making Process

I. Identify Self-Components	II. Explore Career Alternatives	III. Choose Career Option
Related to	Considering	Considering
1. Values	1. Characteristics of work	1. Needs
2. Interests	2. Work conditions	2. Self-assessment
3. Skills and abilities	3. Training and qualifications	3. Career information
4. Self-esteem	4. Employers	4. Alternatives
5. Career maturity	5. Advancement	5. Ranking of preferences
6. Work motivations	6. Employment outlook	6. Reality of preferences
7. Hobbies/activities	7. Earnings	7. Achievement of life goals
8. Life goals	8. Personal interests	

Figure 4.1 provides a rating chart that may further enhance the understanding of how the basic major or career decision-making model operates. In this model the individual lists her or his personal characteristics, including values, work motivators (the direct factors related to environmental conditions that an individual identifies as personally motivating in their work; e.g., working outdoors or with people), interests, abilities and skills, hobbies, activities, and goals in the rows on the left side of chart. In the columns toward the top of the chart the individual lists occupations that are of personal interest. Then, if the individual has an acceptable knowledge of personal characteristics and is well informed about occupational information, a meaningful rating can be completed. In this chart a 0 is given if there is no match between the occupation and the individual, a 1 if there is some match, and a 2 if there is a good fit. The individual can then weigh different areas of personal characteristics more heavily, if that is desired, or can simply look at totals, determining which characteristics are more important to match than others. A chart such as this serves better as a model of how a decision-making process works than as a functional tool.

Although this model is simplistic, it is consistent with Parson's (1909) model of matching an understanding of oneself and the world of work by a process of "true reasoning." It is a simplistic procedure when compared with the vast amount of information identified in Super's (1990) 14 propositions. Even when some characteristics of individuals are consistent with occupations, however, they may not necessarily want to enter into the occupations for which these characteristics are most appropriate. Many

FIGURE 4.1 Job Rating Chart

Now that you have developed a personal profile and have identified some jobs that you have an interest in, fill out this chart to help you clarify which jobs have the best fit with you. The more knowledge you have about the jobs, the more accurate your rating will be, so, be sure to read about the job options you are considering and to talk to people who know about them. Then, complete the chart.

Consider the job and how it fits with each of the personal characteristics you have identified. If there is no fit between your personal characteristics and the job rate it a 0. If there is some fit, but not the best, rate it a 1. And if there is a good fit between the job and the characteristics, rate it a 2. Then, add up the totals to see which jobs fit you best by your own determination. You may want to give more consideration to one area of personal characteristics than others, such as your values are more important than your interests, so, keep this in mind as you examine your totals.

To keep track of important ideas you might come up with during your rating, place a number in the box and circle it. Then, list the number on another sheet of paper and record your idea. These ideas can be quite important in making that final choice.

OCCUPATION

PERSONAL
CHARACTERISTICS

Values

Subtotals

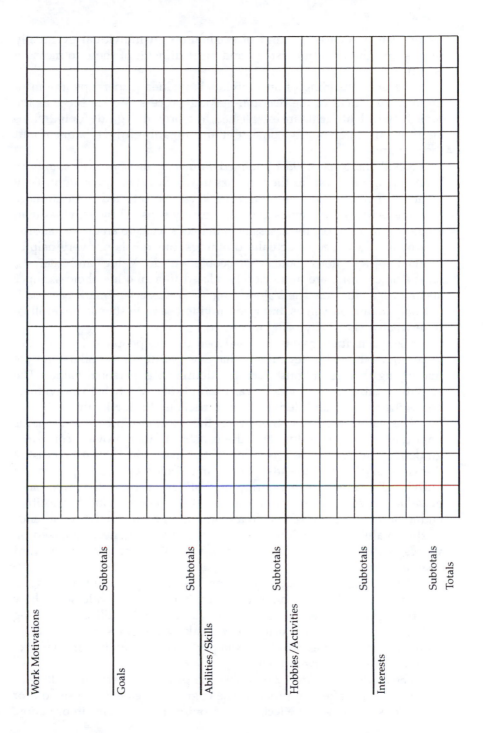

Work Motivations

Subtotals

Goals

Subtotals

Abilities/Skills

Subtotals

Hobbies/Activities

Subtotals

Interests

Subtotals

Totals

factors can influence the kind of occupation an individual eventually selects, and the least understood and most difficult of these to measure is values.

The understanding of an individual's values is, perhaps, the most important element of the decision-making process. Values serve as the basis for which life goals are established, and provide a guide for individuals in making personally consistent and meaningful decisions about their future.

Nevill and Super (1989b) defined values as the objectives sought in behavior, and interests as the activities in which values are sought. They went on to clarify that values and needs can be satisfied through more than one activity, but values are more readily satisfied by activities than are needs. In addition, the assessment of needs leads to an understanding of why and how people actually do things, but this is not very helpful in making predictions about what people will do. Values and interests, on the other hand, are more closely related to actual life choices. Super and Nevill's work on The Values Scale (VS) was a landmark because it not only identified values, but also provided sample statements to illustrate what was actually being measured.

Many activities have been developed to help people list values and to prioritize them, but few, if any, have helped them to understand the underlying themes or constructs that define their personal values. The activity in Table 4.4 is provided as an example of a way to help individuals assess their values and derive the constructs that underlie them.

This values activity demonstrates the relationship between what is important to an individual and the constructs that provide consistent guidance in making decisions in life. The activities in Table 4.4 consist of exercises that help define the underlying constructs that represent an individual's values, a values stripping that demonstrates the importance of values, a feeling comparison exercise to help one establish priorities, and a journaling exercise to help an individual establish the consistency of their values in decision making. As goals are generally based on values, the journaling activity also is a way of noting progress toward goal attainment.

If what makes an individual happy is participating in meaningful life activities and being confirmed, then it is easy to understand how identifying what is meaningful, or one's values, can be utilized in making virtually every decision. Furthermore, making decisions that are in line with what one believes in or feels is important can result in self-reinforcement and a sense of confirmation.

The model in Figure 4.2 describes the process of decision making as a cognitive and affective process. The cognitive elements consist of, for example, knowledge, intellect, the reasoning process, and information,

TABLE 4.4   Values and Decisions

Values are those elements of life that are important to you. If you know them, decision making is a lot easier. Defining your values is sometimes difficult because each person's are unique.

You can use your feelings to help define your personal values. Just ask yourself this question: What would your life be like without the thing in question? For example, what would your life be like without your family? Without money? Without success? Without respect? Would it feel bad? Would you work to have and protect it? If the answers are yes, then you have identified a value.

THIS EXERCISE WILL HELP IDENTIFY AND PRIORITIZE YOUR VALUES.

1. Examine the following list of values and underline the ones you consider important.

Freedom	Justice	Physical activity
Leisure time	Wisdom	Personal development
Independence	Wealth	Social interaction
Honesty	Religion	Helping others
Status	Health	Satisfaction
Respect	Loyalty	Achievement
Honor	Family	Success
Autonomy	Security	Advancement
Morality	Variety	Environment
Art	Power	Peace of mind
Creativity	Fame	Adventure

2. Add other values that you may not have found on the list.
3. When you have completed the list, place the words into groups based upon those that you feel should be in the same category. As you initially place these words into groups, you really don't have to be aware of the common theme that puts them into the same category. As you finish the grouping, however, define the themes that connect these words. The themes represent your true values. Subsequently, if you like, you can identify words that represent the themes you have identified.
4. Once you have identified your themes that define your values, consider what life would be like without each one. To create a hierarchy of values, those which are most important to those which are less so, simply ask yourself what life is like without one value compared to another one and determine which one has greater effect upon your

(continued)

TABLE 4.4 Continued

life. Compare all possible combinations of your values until you feel that the hierarchy you have arrived at is truly representative of what is most important to you.

5. Keep a written record each day of decisions you made and what values were represented in your decision-making process. Are these consistent with the hierarchy that you determined in step two? If not, what adjustment do you need to make? Continue your daily record until you see that your decisions are representative of your values.

all of which contribute to a primarily conscious process. The affective elements consist of values and feelings.

Although values tend to influence feelings, the difficulty that exists is that they are not the only factor influencing them. The classical example that many college students find applicable is the choice between studying and going to a party, or doing some other pleasurable activity. Why is it that many students choose the pleasurable activity, even when they are aware that, in doing so, they will most likely do poorly on their test? Perhaps it is the immediate gratification of the pleasurable activity, or the anxiety that some people experience related to academia, or maybe an emotional attachment related to someone participating in the pleasurable activity. Whatever the reality is, other factors such as immediate gratification or emotional states also affect feelings.

If feelings are consistent with our values, then one generally has little trouble with making choices that lead toward personally meaningful goals. However, if feelings are inconsistent with one's values and override their cognitions, then one may pursue courses of action that are frustrating and damaging to self-esteem. By raising a student's awareness of his or

FIGURE 4.2 A Model of Decision-Making

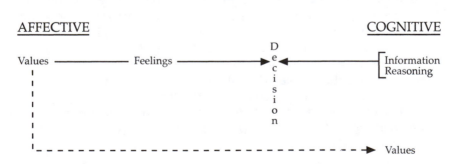

her values, counselors can assist him or her in using them in a more conscious manner as a check against what the individual's feelings actually mean. With increased awareness one also can become aware of what is actually influencing a decision and make clearer choices about pursuing what is congruent with one's values, or that which is incongruent. Helping people understand their values is essential to helping them become good decision makers. And, if counselors are effective at producing good decision makers, they have helped them become better citizens, especially in a free society, and more able to deal with the challenges of life. It also has been observed that helping individuals define themselves, a major task of individuation, further promotes positive mental health by reducing the anxiety one experiences in making poor decisions in life.

In helping individuals define themselves, it is common to run into resistance. The task itself is difficult and takes considerable effort, but there is an even more important reason for individuals to resist defining themselves in this way. As one defines what is important, the individual becomes aware of behaviors and choices that are inconsistent with what they value. To be conscious of making poor choices, or at least those that make it difficult to attain personal goals, confronts a person with his or her own incongruency and works to lower self-esteem. For example, it is quite common for individuals to question themselves following a poor decision and, if the decision leads to painful consequences, the person may experience lowered self-esteem or may even obsess about it and become depressed. If people define what is important, or their values, they become more conscious of the responsibility they have in confirming themselves through acting congruently with what they value. The fact that increasing self-awareness is accompanied by increased responsibility is sometimes difficult for people, but it remains an important step in being able to achieve happiness and the freedom to pursue what is truly important. The resulting resistance to values clarification, however, makes it quite difficult for some people to ever meaningfully determine their identity, except in relation to the institutions to which they belong. Without an understanding of personal values it is difficult to help individuals complete the career decision-making process.

Nevill and Super's (1989b) Values Scale provides a good first step toward defining meaningful work values, but the real task requires considerable introspection and effort toward defining more precisely what is really important to an individual. Table 2.2 identifies and defines the work-related values that Super and Nevill found had internal consistency and appropriate scale independence.

Helping individuals identify their skills and abilities is another important task in defining occupational compatibility. Brown, Brooks, and Associates (1990) indicate that over one-third of the variance in predicting occupational success can be accounted for by knowing only the measured abilities of workers. However, general aptitude tests have been questioned in terms of their utility in assessing one's ability to perform the complex tasks associated with occupations that require college education. Work samples have proven to be a better measure of ability. In addition, many educational and some corporate situations have data already available for admissions, selection, or appraisal programs, and no additional aptitude testing is needed. For these reasons, a general aptitude test is usually not administered as part of the C-DAC battery. Instead, basic skills or abilities checklists are utilized, as they are probably more helpful to college students in helping them identify and organize the skills they want to use in their work. Some of the work sheets from the *Introduction to Type* (Myers, 1993), pertaining to the Myers-Briggs Type Indicator, especially those relating to Effects of Each Preference in Work Situations (see Table 4.5), can be quite helpful in assisting people in defining their preferred skills and abilities. Of course, the best way they can determine if these skills and abilities apply to specific jobs is to gather information concerning the various occupations. Many self-help books include worksheets and activities that assist individuals in identifying the skills and abilities they want to utilize in their career pursuits.

Interests have been defined in numerous ways, most of the definitions having as a basic element liking an activity or object. Interests generally seem to reflect many things, such as gender, family, or social class, and tend to fulfill some level of individual needs. Inventoried interests tend to reflect individual responses to occupations and activities that are compared to various groups of other individuals, for example, those who work in a specific occupation who say they like it whose responses have been statistically analyzed and subsequently serve as norms. The Occupational Scales of the Strong Interest Inventory (SII) (Hansen, 1994) reflect such measured interests. The General Occupational Themes and Basic Interest Scales of the SII add a second dimension as they organize an individual's interests into the areas similar to those defined by Holland (1973) (Figure 4.3). For these reasons the SII is generally utilized as part of the C-DAC assessment battery. The SII has been explained in Chapter 2; it is therefore sufficient to note that it provides an important tool in the process of vocational guidance. However, it is only a tool and, as with other assessments, is no absolute indicator as to which occupation an individual will enjoy or at which he or she will succeed.

The examination of preferred roles in life is another important element to examine in the career counseling process. Discussion of life roles can assist in goal setting by comparing what is significant in the present to what one expects to find significant in the future. The discussion of life roles also can help individuals understand development and the

TABLE 4.5 Myers-Briggs Type Indicators Effects of Preferences in Work Situations

EXTRAVERSION	INTROVERSION
Like variety and action	Like quiet for concentration
Often impatient with long, slow jobs	Tend not to mind working on one project for a long time uninterruptedly
Are interested in the activities of their work and in how other people do it	Are interested in the facts/ideas behind their work
Often act quickly, sometimes without thinking	Like to think a lot before they act, sometimes without acting
Develop ideas by discussion	Develop ideas by reflection
Like having people around	Like working alone with no interruptions
Learn new tasks by talking and doing	Learn new tasks by reading and reflecting

SENSING	INTUITION
Like using experience and standard ways to solve problems	Like solving new complex problems
Enjoy applying what they have already learned	Enjoy learning a new skill more than using it
May distrust and ignore their inspirations	Will follow their inspirations
Seldom make errors of fact	May ignore or overlook facts
Like to do things with a practical bent	Like to do things with an innovative bent
Like to present the details of their work first	Like to present an overview of their work first
Prefer continuation of what is, with fine tuning	Prefer change, sometimes radical, to continuation of what is
Usually proceed step-by-step	Usually proceed in bursts of energy

(continued)

TABLE 4.5 Continued

THINKING	FEELING
Use logical analysis to reach conclusions	Use values to reach conclusions
Want mutual respect among colleagues	Want harmony and support among colleagues
May hurt people's feelings without knowing it	Enjoy pleasing people, even in unimportant things
Tend to decide impersonally, sometimes paying insufficient attention to people's wishes	Often let decisions be influenced by their own and other people's likes and dislikes
Tend to be firm-minded and can give criticism when appropriate	Tend to be sympathetic and dislike, even avoid, telling people unpleasant things
Look at the principles involved in the situation	Look at the underlying values in the situation
Feel rewarded when job is done well	Feel rewarded when people's needs are met

JUDGING	PERCEIVING
Work best when they can plan their work and follow their plan	Enjoy flexibility in their work
Like to get things settled and finished	Like to leave things open for last-minute changes
May not notice new things that need to be done	May postpone unpleasant tasks that need to be done
Tend to be satisfied once they reach a decision on a thing, situation, or person	Tend to be curious and welcome a new light on a thing, situation, or person
Reach closure by deciding quickly	Postpone decisions while searching for options
Feel supported by structure and schedules	Adapt well to changing situations and feel restricted without variety
Focus on completion of a project	Focus on the process of a project

FIGURE 4.3 Holland's Hexagonal Model

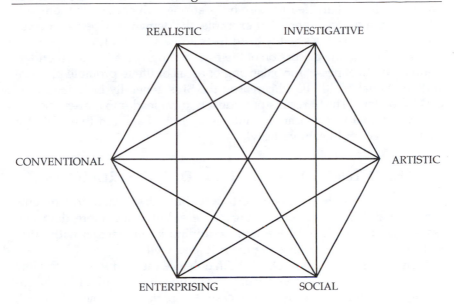

Realistic type: a preference for activities that entail the explicit, ordered, or systematic manipulation of objects, tools, machines, and animals; and an aversion to educational or therapeutic activity.

Investigative type: a preference for activities that entail the observational, symbolic, systematic, and creative investigation of physical, biological, and cultural phenomena in order to understand such phenomena; and an aversion to persuasive, social, and repetitive activities.

Artistic type: a preference for ambiguous, free, unsystematized activities that entail the manipulation of physical, verbal, or human materials to create artforms or products; and an aversion to explicit, systematic, and ordered activities.

Social type: preference for activities that entail the manipulation of others to inform, train, develop, cure, or enlighten; and an aversion to explicit, ordered, systematic activities involving materials, tools, or machines.

Enterprising type: a preference for activity that entails the manipulation of others to attain organizational gains or economic gains; and an aversion to observational, symbolic, and systematic activities.

Conventional type: a preference for activities that entail explicit, ordered, systematic manipulation of data, such as keeping records, filing materials, reproducing materials, organizing written and numerical data according to a prescribed plan, operating business machines and data processing machines to attain organizational or economic goals; and an aversion to ambiguous, free, exploratory, or unsystematized activities.

changes that they will go through as they grow older. Of course, the preference for certain life roles also has a strong influence on the compatibility of certain occupations. For example, the demands of being a doctor can severely affect one's ability to address home and family as a preferred role. In addition, the discussion of life roles naturally leads into an understanding of "wellness," the balancing of areas of life to promote physical and emotional health. For this reason the SI is generally included in the C-DAC battery. The SI results provide a natural lead into a discussion of how vocational and avocational interests can be balanced to establish a well-rounded and healthy lifestyle.

THE INTERACTION OF THE C-DAC INSTRUMENTS

It has already been illustrated how various assessment instruments can facilitate the career counseling process, but using more than one assessment can be helpful through examining its interaction with other instruments, and the counseling interview as well.

The different sections of the SII can enhance the counseling interview process and subsequently help in understanding the individual. For example, if scores are similar on the General Occupational Themes of the SII, the results yield a "flat profile." The resulting lack of differentiation may be related to low career maturity, or may be a reflection of the need for considerable variety in his or her occupational choice. The Career Development Inventory (CDI) may shed more light as to which alternative interpretation is more likely to be accurate.

The Administrative Indexes of the SII can serve to identify several issues for further inquiry. If there are a large percentage of "Like" or "Dislike" responses to Occupations and/or School Subjects, it may suggest, as with the "flat profile," that the individual is undifferentiated in his or her occupational choices. In any case, a large percentage of "Like" responses to these two areas will provide numerous alternatives for an individual to research. In a similar manner, if the percentage of "Like" responses on the Characteristics section is low, it may reflect a negative self-esteem in relation to work, another area that can only be confirmed or rejected through the counseling interview.

Additional questions can be generated by looking at the Basic Interest Scales and determining how interests inconsistent with preferred Occupational Themes may influence the individual's perception of working in certain occupations. For example, how can an individual meet his or her interests identified in the Adventure Basic Interest scales when Conventional is his or her highest Occupational Theme?

The CDI can help in several other very explicit ways. For example, it can suggest if the individual has the attitudes and knowledge to make a meaningful choice. If the individual ranks low in comparison to others his or her own age and educational level, how ready is he or she to make a meaningful choice? With low percentile ranks it is logical to question if the results of other tests related to career choice, such as the SII, are even meaningful. How can one who has done little career planning, and/ or has little knowledge about the world of work and what it takes to succeed in jobs, be ready to make any kind of meaningful choice? The results of the CDI may simply suggest that the individual needs to learn more about the world of work and himself or herself before any other testing is appropriate. Therefore, it is easy to see how this instrument may be the best to administer first in any series of career-related tests.

The Salience Inventory (SI) also can facilitate the counseling interview. For example, how consistent is the order of preference of the different roles among the Participation, Commitment, and Values Expectation sections of the SI? It would be expected that work and study may shift between the Participation and Commitment or Values Expectation sections, but other inconsistencies provide a basis for questions as to what the individual expects to change in his or her life.

The VS is equally helpful in its capacity to enhance the counseling interview. The values identified by the VS can lead to questions about responses on the SII and SI. For example, how can the VS values identified in the VS be realized in the occupations identified as similar in the SII, or how do the VS preferred values relate to the various preferred roles derived from the SI?

It is easy to see how responses on any one of the C-DAC instruments may lead to questions about responses on other instruments, or to additional questions, thus enhancing the counseling interview. Research is currently being accomplished that will show more concrete interactions between the four primary instruments used in the C-DAC battery. The results of this research will add other insights about a battery of tests that already provides significant assistance to individuals in the career choice process.

CAREER COUNSELING SERVICES IN COLLEGES AND UNIVERSITIES

After having examined the C-DAC model from the vantage point of the counseling interview and various assessment instruments, it may prove helpful to look at how it would fit into a model of services in a college or university.

There are numerous models for the provision of career counseling services in universities and colleges, each one generally following a particular evolutionary history. However, most of them contain some or all of the following components:

1. A career resource center that has materials such as:
   a) general resource books, such as *The Complete Guide for Occupational Exploration* (Farr, 1993), *The Dictionary of Occupational Titles 4th Edition* (U.S. Department of Labor, 1991), and *The Occupational Outlook Handbook 1996–1997 Edition* (U.S. Department of Labor, 1996);
   b) more specific career resource books, such as the VGM series;
   c) occupational files that include informational pamphlets from professional organizations, newspapers, and magazines;
   d) computerized career guidance systems, such as SIGI-PLUS (1985) and DISCOVER (1984);
   e) information from individuals who are in the various occupations, whether it be from a source such as *Vocational Biographies* (1994), a resource list of alumni who have graduated from the university, or simply a resource list of individuals from within the community.
2. Vocational assessment, such as the SII, the CDI, the SI, or the VS.
3. Professional counselors or psychologists who have been trained in career counseling.
4. Placement centers that focus on interviewing and resume-writing skills, and also provide contacts for direct employment.
5. Courses that focus on teaching the career development process, including activities on developing self-awareness, education on how to access and utilize career information resources, and decision making (Osborne & Usher, 1994).

Career resource centers are essential in any setting where there are individuals seeking information about the world of work at some stage of making a decision concerning their major or an occupational choice. These resources may be in one office or several, but all play an important role in assisting students with the career development process. According to Zunker (1990), the advantages of career resource centers include:

1. All career materials can be organized into efficient and workable units in a central location, thus facilitating the administrative tasks of monitoring and upgrading of these materials.
2. Students, faculty, and staff are more likely to make use of an attractive, accessible central location that has career-related programs as its focus.
3. The presence of an organized career resource center invites interaction; that is, students and faculty are more likely to assist with development and programming when career information is visible, easily accessible, and centrally located. When career planning

programming and information are scattered throughout the institution, faculty may be reluctant to participate simply because they do not know where to go for which data.

4. A corollary of this last point is the ease with which outreach activities can be generated. Because the career resource center is a self-contained source of information, new directions and needed activities are easier to ascertain and mobilize.

Raskin (1987) suggests that career resource centers provide two specific kinds of information:

1. Components that promote effective career planning such as materials that teach career decision making, instruments of vocational assessment, aids to job search skill development, and job simulations; and

2. Specific information resource components, such as occupational descriptions and projections; educational and training information, information about military service, apprenticeships, and internships; and resource persons who can be contacted for further information.

As the career development process is lifelong, it is quite common for students to return to utilize resource centers well after their educational goals have been attained, and this is one more way in which colleges and universities can provide a continuing service to both their clientele and the society as a whole.

Vocational assessment, which ethically can only be provided by trained counselors or psychologists, is another service that provides significant assistance to college students as they choose a major or career direction. Courses that assist undecided students with these same decisions generally utilize both career resource centers and vocational assessment as part of the curriculum (Osborne & Usher, 1994). Subsequent utilization of the services of a campus placement center can assist the student with implementing a job search upon graduation.

AN EXAMPLE OF CAREER COUNSELING SERVICES AT ONE UNIVERSITY

It would not be feasible to describe the numerous ways in which career counseling services are organized at different institutions; however, illustrating how services are organized at one university may be helpful.

The institution chosen for this purpose is a large, land grant university that has provided substantial resources to assist its students and alumni in the area of career development. The career development services at this institution are provided in three different offices at this university: Advising, Career Planning and Placement, and Counseling and Testing.

The various advising offices, located in the different colleges, assist students in a minimal way in choosing majors. The function of these offices is more focused on course selection and assisting students in accessing the resources that they need, one area being career development.

The Career Planning and Placement Center (CPP) provides numerous services in relation to helping students with interview and resume-writing skills, and in the job placement arena. In addition, the CPP offers a credit course that briefly describes the career development process, but focuses much more time on job placement skills.

The office that focuses on providing students and, to a limited extent, alumni with career development services is the Counseling and Testing Center (C&T). The C&T has numerous services that are available to assist in the career development process. When students first approach C&T, they are asked to complete an informational packet that includes some basic demographic data, some elements of employment history, and asks them to describe the concerns for which they are seeking services. The students subsequently are asked to attend a 1-hour Career Orientation Seminar (COS) to find out more about the services that are available. The COS has three primary goals:

1. to briefly educate students as to the career decision-making process,
2. to educate students as to the variety of resources that they can utilize, and
3. to help match the students with the resources most appropriate for their concerns.

Students can choose from a variety of resources and services, including a well-organized and comprehensive career information center, a variety of one-session assessment interpretation groups, the computerized career decision-making systems SIGI-PLUS or DISCOVER, or they may make an appointment with a counseling psychologist who has been trained in career development. Many of the services, such as the career information center or the computerized decision-making programs, can be utilized by students without the assistance of counseling staff. The assessment interpretation groups and the individual counseling services are provided by the counseling psychologists. In addition, students may attend single-session outreach programs that focus on career development issues. When students choose to participate in an assessment-related group, they have several options.

The first option, especially appropriate for students who are in early exploration, is a group that utilizes the Harrington-O'Shea System for Career Decision Making-Revised (1992). To begin the group, the students are administered the Harrington-O'Shea, which has several advantages. The primary advantages of this instrument are:

1. it is self scoring;
2. it generates a number of occupational options;
3. the levels of training programs are identified, for example, apprenticeship or on-the-job training, vocational school, 2-year college, or college;
4. the employment outlook is identified in a general manner;
5. it helps orient the individual to considering other elements important to career decision making, including values and abilities;
6. the results have a high correlation with those of the SII, and
7. once preferred occupations are identified, there are cross references to the *Dictionary of Occupational Titles* (U.S. Department of Labor, 1991) and *The Complete Guide for Occupational Exploration* (Farr, 1993), which promotes the generation of additional alternatives.

Following the administration of the Harrington-O'Shea, students are given the opportunity to work in the Career Information Center with the guidance of a counseling psychologist. Group size is limited to provide for individualized attention. Students are given hands-on instruction as to how to conduct an alternative search, one that identifies multiple options related to occupations they are considering, and are assisted in using other resources in the Career Information Center. Following the group, students may pursue a career search of their own, participate in additional assessment groups, or sign up for individualized counseling, if they desire.

The second option, a variety of groups offering interpretations of different assessment instruments, appeals to students who have completed at least some exploration and are moving into confirming their initial impressions. This option is most relevant for students who are in late Exploration or in early Establishment, and involves using Super's stages to illustrate the client's developmental level (see Figure 1.1). The assessment options include:

1. The SII,
2. A combination assessment group of the SII and the Myers-Briggs Type Indicator (MBTI),
3. The C-DAC battery, which consists of the SII, the CDI, the SI, and the VS.

One and one-half to 2-hour interpretation sessions are provided for each of these groups. Students may pursue other resource options, such as individual counseling, following the interpretive group. Students may access any of the options through individual counseling as well, including the C-DAC battery.

An option that is comprehensive and covers many factors related to career choice is the utilization of one of the computerized career decision-making programs. Although there are many computerized career assistance programs to choose from, for example, a Career Information System (CIS), the Guidance Information System (GIS), and others, SIGI-PLUS and DISCOVER are two of the best known and will be discussed more extensively, because they are those currently used in the C&T.

SIGI-PLUS consists of nine sections including an Introduction, Self-Assessment, Search, Information, Skills, Preparing, Coping, Deciding, and Next Steps. The Self-Assessment section focuses on helping an individual identify meaningful work-related values and interests. The Search section helps one identify occupations that match the individual's values and interests in a career and demonstrates the relation between specific college majors and the occupations to which they can lead. The Information section provides information about various occupations and allows the individual to ask questions about the occupations. The specific skills that an individual needs to succeed in an occupation are identified in the Skills section. The training that is required and details about where to get the training are included in the Preparing section. The last three sections, Coping, Deciding, and Next Steps, help an individual evaluate the risks and steps that will lead an individual into an occupation. SIGI-PLUS is an excellent program that helps educate the user about elements that are consistently important in career choice and development. At the same time, the program provides a vast amount of information for the individual to use in determining the compatibility of different occupations.

DISCOVER is similar to SIGI-PLUS in many ways. The program also has nine sections that include the Career Journey Inventory, which identifies the individual's level of career development, and sections on Learning About the World of Work, Learning About Yourself, Finding Occupations, Learning About Occupations, Making Educational Choices, Planning Next Steps, Planning Your Career, and Making Transitions. The section Learning About Yourself includes inventories of interests, abilities, values, and other personal information. This section also allows one to enter scores from the SII, the Self Directed Search, or the Career Decision Making System. Two sections, Finding Occupations and Learning About Occupations, help the individual identify compatible occupations and gather information about them. Training programs and college information are included in the Making Educational Choices section and in the Planning Next Steps section. Additional personal considerations are evaluated in the last two sections, Planning Your Career and Making Transitions. Both SIGI-PLUS and DISCOVER provide helpful information for individuals and counselors to use in the career counseling process.

Following the COS, a student may choose to work with an individual counselor. The counselors have all had both coursework and supervised experiences in the provision of career counseling services. Working with an individual counselor, students may take additional assessment instruments or may involve themselves in self-exploration. Counselors also may assist in helping an individual understand the decision-making process more effectively or in a number of other ways.

The services at C&T have been developed to assist a large number of individuals with a limited staff. The COS serves to get individuals started and helps connect them with appropriate materials and services. In some cases, students who would not access a counselor do considerable work on their own once they have learned how to use the resources in the Career Information Center.

This example of the career-related services provided by a major university counseling center demonstrates the resources that are helpful, if not necessary, to provide comprehensive assistance to students. The role of the C-DAC model and its innovative assessment is clearly illustrated through the group interpretations of assessment instruments, individual counseling, the career information center, and even the computerized career assistance programs. The developmental nature of these services is illustrated through the initial provision of basic information that leads to increasingly specific information concerning decision making and career alternatives. The numerous service-related options provide multiple ways for students to get involved in their own search and to supplement their first step with subsequent options. The options are combined in a way that provides for a solid base of information about self, the world of work, and the compatibility between the two. Once learned, the process may be duplicated throughout life as changes in the individual and the world of work occur.

Following are case studies demonstrating the use of the C-DAC model with three clients: Linda, an 18-year-old college freshman; David, a 36-year-old dentist; and Jane, a 21-year-old college senior.

THE CASE OF LINDA

Linda was an 18-year-old freshman who came into the counseling center to receive help in determining her major. Her father and mother were successful entrepreneurs, and she came from an upper-middle-class background. Although Linda had been quite active in high school activities, she had no previous work experience. Linda indicated that she had a high grade point average in high school, and that she didn't need to work very hard to attain it. She also indicated that there had been a number of teachers in her extended family, but that she really did not see herself as a teacher, because of her discomfort in handling discipline problems. Linda did, however, express an interest in becoming a doctor, but demonstrated low awareness as to what a physician's lifestyle encompassed.

Initially, Linda was given a number of activities to help identify her values, skills, and abilities, and instructions on how to do an alternative search utilizing Career Information Center materials to identify occupations of interest. Upon her return a week later, she had done very little in terms of completing any of the activities, or in using the Career Information Center to identify occupations that interested her. Instead, she had participated in numerous leisure activities. This session was the first of many to follow, and established a pattern of erratic sessions and little effort on her part to complete any task that would help her to determine a meaningful major. In addition, the work in each session reflected an individual who was immature and not ready to make a meaningful choice. Efforts to help Linda define herself in terms of self-concept were met with resistance. When confronted with the resistance, Linda would indicate that the work was difficult and she had never been required to consider the areas that were the focus of the current work. Subsequently, she would change the focus of the session to personal relationships. The C-DAC battery, consisting of the SII, the CDI, the SI, and the VS, were not administered in the initial phase of counseling, as it may have inappropriately influenced Linda by giving her some easy answers.

After several sessions of little progress, Linda was instructed to only make another appointment after she had at least worked on SIGI-PLUS or DISCOVER, the computerized career decision-making programs. SIGI-PLUS and DISCOVER tend to be difficult for individuals with low self-awareness, because they define options that often are incompatible with the individual's perceptions of what he or she wants. This result was precisely what Linda obtained. At her next appointment she indicated that none of the options that had been presented were of interest to her. She was then instructed to make subsequent appointments with SIGI-PLUS until she understood what factors of self-concept would lead her to more attractive occupations. As Linda used the computerized program, she increasingly began identifying elements of her own self-concept that were important, as well as occupational alternatives. She also continued to discuss relationship and family issues. These discussions led her to an insight about how dependent she had been on her parents and other significant others to make decisions for her. As a result, she decided to spend more time identifying her own values.

As Linda became more aware of herself, she also was working to identify occupational alternatives. In the middle of her sophomore year, following considerable work and a number of periods where she had not participated in counseling, Linda seemed to be at a point where the utilization of the C-DAC battery would be helpful to her.

Linda's C-DAC Results

Career Development Inventory
(College Form)

(Percentile Scores)

Career Planning 90
Career Exploration 99
Decision-Making 81
World-of-Work Information 23
Career Development Attitudes 99
Career Development Knowledge 55
Career Orientation Total 99
Knowledge of Preferred
   Occupation 70
(Social Science, Teaching / Social Service)

Strong Interest Inventory

Academic Comfort 41
Introversion-Extroversion 32

Themes:
Social .... Very High 69
Enterprising .... Very High 65
Conventional .... Average 55
Artistic .... Average 53
Realistic .... Average 46
Investigative .... Low 36

Basic Interest Scales:
Very High: Medical Service 69
              Athletics 63
High: Medical Science 61
              Writing 63
              Teaching 63
              Public Speaking 62
              Merchandising 64
              Business Management 60

Occupations:
Very Similar: Flight Attendant 65
              Broadcaster 57
              YWCA / YWCA Director 60
              Realtor 55

(continued)

99

Similar:	Public Relations Director	50
	English Teacher	50
	Personnel Director	49
	Store Manager	54
	Purchasing Agent	45
	Buyer	47
	Advertising Executive	50

(24 similar occupations, mostly in Social and Enterprising)

The Values Scale

(Ratings Range from 1 = Low to 4 = High)

4.0	Achievement
4.0	Economic Security
4.0	Working Conditions
3.8	Creativity
3.8	Cultural Identity
3.8	Economic Rewards
3.8	Personal Development
3.8	Variety
3.6	Social Interaction
3.6	Social Relations
3.4	Advancement
3.4	Life Style
3.2	Ability Utilization
3.2	Altruism
3.2	Authority
3.2	Autonomy
3.0	Aesthetics
2.8	Prestige
2.4	Physical Activity
1.6	Physical Prowess
1.2	Risk

The Salience Inventory

(Ratings Range from 1 = Low to 4 = High)

	Study	Work	Community Service	Home & Family	Leisure Activities
Participation	3.2	2.4	2.0	3.5	3.8
Commitment	2.7	2.7	2.9	4.0	3.9
Values Expectations	2.5	3.3	2.7	3.6	3.6

Using the C-DAC Battery With Linda

Linda's SII results suggested an interest in Social and Enterprising occupations. These two General Occupational Themes were rated as Very High. Her Basic Interest Scales also supported a number of Social and Enterprising thematic areas, and emphasized medical service, athletics, and medical science. The Occupational Scales identified four very similar and 24 similar occupations, most of which also came from Social and Enterprising thematic areas. In addition, Linda's Academic Comfort score was about average for an individual graduating with a bachelor's degree, and her Introversion-Extroversion score indicated that she was quite extroverted.

The CDI suggested that Linda's involvement in career planning, as evidenced by her ability to find good career-related resources and use decision-making knowledge and skills, should contribute to making a decision concerning her choice of major. However, her knowledge about occupations seemed to be lower than that of her peers. This finding suggested that Linda still needed to explore occupational alternatives before making a decision. It was not surprising that Linda's knowledge of Social Science, Teaching, and Social Service occupations was relatively high due to the number of individuals in her family that had been in teaching-related careers.

On the SI, Linda indicated that she was currently most invested in Leisure Activities and Home/Family, both roles consistently elevated above the others, now and in the future. In the future, Linda expected to place more time into work than into study, which may be explained by her expectation of moving from being a student into the work force. This shift between the Participation and Values Expectations levels of the SI is quite common with college students. It also was clear that Linda felt that Community Service was more important than she reflected by her present activities, and that she would invest more time in it in the future. Overall, the SI demonstrated consistency between the levels of Participation, Commitment, and Values Expectations if one allows for the age-appropriate shifts in Study and Work and Community Service.

Linda had eight values on the VS that were rated high, 3.8 or 4.0, with the remaining values significantly lower. There was a mixture of values representing an intrinsic and extrinsic emphasis, but two of her values rated 4.0, Economic Security and Working conditions, were extrinsic. Her top-rated intrinsic value was Achievement. Most of the values that Linda rated 3.8 were intrinsic: Creativity, Cultural Identity, Personal Development, and Variety. Her one extrinsic value rated at 3.8 was Economic Security.

Looking at the C-DAC test instruments together, Linda's SII results seemed quite consistent with earlier expressed interests. The occupations reflected in the Occupational Scales were similar to alternatives that she previously had identified. She confirmed her interests in Social and Enterprising occupational alternatives, as well as interests in Medical Science. The SI reflected her true reasons for not wanting to pursue medical science options, since the only related occupational alternative she expressed an interest in was becoming a medical doctor. Her perceived conflict between the time in schooling and the time she considered she would have to invest in her career was in conflict with the importance she placed on Home/Family and Leisure. She had already expressed very little interest in Social alternatives, as defined by the SII, including teaching. Her perceptions that there were difficult Working Conditions in Social occupations, and that the Economic Rewards were low, were inconsistent with her values, as identified on the VS. Subsequently, Linda was left with Enterprising alternatives. Combining her SII Basic Interests in Writing, Public Speaking, Merchandising, and Business Management, Linda explored related alternatives and eventually declared a major in marketing. She felt that this was consistent with all of her preferred values, allowed for adequate time for Home/Family and Leisure pursuits, and was consistent with her interests.

Following her junior year, Linda indicated that she was enjoying her marketing coursework. In order to provide a greater level of security that she was pursuing the right career track, Linda decided to complete a cooperative education experience with a marketing firm during her senior year. After completing this experience, she reported that the marketing field was very exciting, rewarding, and consistent with virtually everything that she had determined she wanted. Upon graduation from the university, Linda returned to a full-time position with the marketing firm that she had worked for during her cooperative education experience. At last report, Linda indicated that she continued to be quite happy with her choice.

THE CASE OF DAVID

David was a 36-year-old successful dentist who returned to the counseling center to explore more satisfying occupational alternatives. He lived in a small town close to the university, and had been taking courses in the evenings in an attempt to find an area that would capture his interests. He recently had been divorced and was dealing with his changing role as a parent, along with continued hostility from his ex-wife. David's main complaints about being a dentist in general practice were unhappy patients and feeling required to perform a variety of procedures that he felt competent with, but at which he was not an expert. He also was feeling financial pressure as a result of the divorce settlement.

At the initial meeting it was clear that David was having problems with situational depression that seemed to be exacerbated by dissatisfaction with his current occupation. Due to the limited amount of time that David had available, the C-DAC battery was administered following the initial interview. As it seemed clear that David had reentered the Exploration stage of Super's developmental schema, the CDI was administered instead of the ACCI in order to ensure that he had the knowledge base, skills and abilities, and attitudes that were appropriate to make a good career decision. The highest norms for the CDI in relation to age and educational level were utilized, even though they were not commensurate with his age or level of educational attainment.

David's C-DAC Results

Career Development Inventory
(College Form)

(Percentile Scores)

Career Planning	70
Career Exploration	73
Decision-Making	63
World-of-Work Information	69
Career Development Attitudes	84
Career Development Knowledge	67
Career Orientation Total	83
Knowledge of Preferred Occupation	55

(Biological and Medical Science)

Strong Interest Inventory

Academic Comfort	50
Introversion-Extroversion	49

Themes:

Realistic	High	65
Investigative	Mod. High	60
Social	Mod. High	57
Enterprising	Mod. High	57
Artistic	Average	53
Conventional	Average	45

Basic Interest Scales:

Very High:	Nature	64
High:	Military Activities	70
	Religious	62
	Medical Service	59
	Domestic Arts	55

(continued)

Average:	Athletics	58
	Science	55
	Teaching	54
	Business Management	54

Occupations:

Very Similar:	Dentist	56
	Chiropractor	50
	Pharmacist	48
	Medical Technologist	49
	Respiratory Therapist	54
	Physical Therapist	45
Similar:	Veterinarian	46
	Police Officer	45
Moderately Similar:	(15, mostly in Realistic, Investigative, and Social)	

The Values Scale

(Ratings Range from 1 = Low to 4 = High)

3.6 .... Personal Development
3.2 .... Achievement
3.0 .... Social Relations
2.8 .... Ability Utilization
2.8 .... Lifestyle
2.8 .... Economic Security
2.6 .... Working Conditions
2.6 .... Creativity
2.6 .... Aesthetics
2.4 .... Autonomy
2.2 .... Advancement
2.2 .... Altruism
2.2 .... Authority
2.2 .... Variety
2.0 .... Economic Rewards
2.0 .... Physical Activity
2.0 .... Prestige
2.0 .... Social Interaction
2.0 .... Cultural Identity
1.4 .... Risk
1.4 .... Physical Prowess

The Salience Inventory

(Ratings Range from 1 = Low to 4 = High)

	Study	Work	Community Service	Home & Family	Leisure Activities
Participation	2.1	2.9	1.6	3.1	2.3
Commitment	2.7	3.2	2.9	4.0	3.0
Values Expectations	2.5	2.8	2.4	2.6	2.7

Using the C-DAC Battery With David

David's score on the SII Academic Comfort scale reflected that he was about average for an individual pursuing a master's degree. His Introversion-Extroversion scale score suggested that he liked elements of both working with others and on his own in non-people-related tasks. The Realistic General Occupational Theme was rated as high, with three others being moderately high: Investigative, Social, and Enterprising. Nature, more of an avocational interest than a vocational one, was identified as a very similar Basic Interest Scale with Military Activities, Religious Activities, Medical Service, and Domestic Arts receiving a high rating. On the Occupational Scales, Dentist was rated as being "Very Similar" and Veterinarian, Police Officer, Chiropractor, Pharmacist, Medical Technologist, Respiratory Therapist, and Physical Therapist all received "Similar" ratings. The overall SII results were very consistent with David's current occupational choice of being a dentist.

The results of the CDI suggested that David had adequate knowledge and skills to have made a meaningful occupational choice. The only scale that provided some question was his average knowledge in relation to his preferred occupational group, Biological and Medical Science.

The results of the SI were quite interesting. The overall pattern indicated that he felt all five life roles were more important to him, as reflected by his Commitment score, than either his current involvement, Participation, or his future investment, Values Expectation, indicated. In all areas except Home/Family the difference between his Participation and Values Expectation scores reflected that he expected to be doing more in the future than he currently was. In relation to his Home/Family score, although it was his highest level of Commitment, he expected to be doing less in the future than he currently was. This result may have been indicative of his recent divorce and difficulty with his new status as a noncustodial father.

David's most important values, as supported by the results of the VS, were intrinsic and related to Personal Development and Achievement. These results were consistent with his continuing to attend the university, even after having completed his training as a dentist, and his dissatisfaction with his current occupation. Most of his other preferred values were also intrinsic, with the exception of Economic Security and Working Conditions. The importance of Economic Security seemed quite consistent with his new financial difficulties, and Working Conditions might reflect the dissatisfaction with his current employment.

The C-DAC battery leads to several important conclusions. The SII results were consistent with David's current occupational choice, and were supported as being valid by the results of the CDI. The relatively high scores on the CDI demonstrated that David had the skills and knowledge to make a meaningful choice. The fact that Dentist was the only "Very Similar" occupation indicated by the SII Occupational Scales was clear confirmation of his vocational choice. The average score on the Knowledge of Preferred Occupation scale of the CDI suggested that David needed to explore more alternatives related to his current occupation.

This search of occupations and specialties within his current occupation was contracted for as part of the counseling process and was subsequently very thoroughly accomplished. The basic pattern reflected by the SI was consistent across the scales, with the exception of Home/Family. The high Commitment score on Home/Family was in contrast to scores on the same role in both the Participation and Values Expectations scales. In discussing this with David, the contrast seemed to reflect how important Home/Family was to him, his current distress about his divorce and separation from his children, and his pessimistic outlook that the relationship would not improve enough to allow him more contact with his children and ex-wife. This discussion, along with his verification of other depressive symptoms, led to some work on treating the depression and a later referral to a more convenient therapist for continued treatment. As the occupational search was increasingly separated from his therapeutic work, David began identifying specialties in dentistry that would lead to a more specialized practice, a higher income, and improved relations with his clients. As counseling was terminated, David indicated that he had been accepted into a specialty program at his previous dental professional school, and was planning on becoming an endodontist. He believed this to be a very positive option that was consistent with all of his values as indicated by the VS.

THE CASE OF JANE

Jane was a 21-year-old, single woman who came to counseling because she was unsure of her major in journalism. Jane was a college senior who was finding that some aspects of a career in journalism did not appeal to her, yet she was afraid that changing majors would delay her graduation. In particular, she did not like the level of competition among her student peers who shared the same major, and perceived them to be quite aggressive. She also was concerned about the low availability of good-paying jobs that were available upon graduation, and the competition for positions that this created. Jane currently was working part-time in a telemarketing firm. She indicated that her job was not very enjoyable, but that she did find pleasure in her interactions with other employees. She had previous work experience as a retail salesperson in a clothing store, and as a waitress. Because Jane was concerned about graduation, she had considered going to graduate school in law or psychology.

Upon entering into counseling, Jane indicated that she really was not sure what she wanted to do, but that she was sure she did not want to continue in journalism. She expressed that she had received no previous career counseling. Because Jane wanted information quickly and due to the fact that graduation was near, she was given the C-DAC battery.

Jane's C-DAC Results

Career Development Inventory
(College Form)

(Percentile Scores)
Career Planning	08
Career Exploration	52
Decision-Making	03
World-of-Work Information	27
Career Development Attitudes	15
Career Development Knowledge	06
Career Orientation Total	04
Knowledge of Preferred Occupation	39
(Art and Music)	

Strong Interest Inventory

Academic Comfort	44
Introversion-Extroversion	46

Themes:
Social	Mod. High	61
Artistic	Average	58
Investigative	Average	50
Conventional	Average	47
Realistic	Average	45
Enterprising	Very Low	38

Basic Interest Scales:
Very High:	Adventure	63
High:	Art	64
	Religious Activities	64
Moderately High:	Music/Drama	61
	Social Service	60
	Domestic Arts	62
	Law/Politics	56
Moderately Low:	Nature	43
	Medical Science	43
	Merchandising	39
	Business Management	38

(continued)

Occupations:

Very Similar:	Police Officer	45
	Art Teacher	48
	Musician	45
	Flight Attendant	51
	Advertising Executive	45
	Special Education Teacher	48
Similar:	Photographer	42
	Broadcaster	43
	Guidance Counselor	42

The Values Scale

(Ratings Range from 1 = Low to 4 = High)

4.0 .... Achievement
3.8 .... Ability Utilization
3.4 .... Creativity
3.4 .... Personal Development
3.2 .... Prestige
3.2 .... Social Relations
3.2 .... Economic Security
2.8 .... Advancement
2.8 .... Economic Rewards
2.8 .... Working Conditions
2.6 .... Aesthetics
2.6 .... Life Style
2.6 .... Social Interaction
2.4 .... Altruism
2.4 .... Cultural Identity
2.2 .... Variety
2.0 .... Authority
2.0 .... Physical Activity
1.8 .... Autonomy
1.2 .... Physical Prowess
1.2 .... Risk

The Salience Inventory

(Ratings Range from 1 = Low to 4 = High)

	Study	Work	Community Service	Home & Family	Leisure Activities
Participation	3.4	2.1	1.7	3.4	3.0
Commitment	3.7	3.1	1.8	4.0	2.9
Values Expectations	3.1	3.1	2.1	3.4	2.9

Using the C-DAC Battery With Jane

The SII suggested that Jane was relatively comfortable in the academic environment for a college senior. This result was supported by her score on the Academic Comfort Scale, which is about average for an individual with a bachelor's degree. Her score on the Introversion-Extroversion Scale indicated that she enjoyed a combination of working with people and with inanimate things as well. The highest General Occupational Theme for Jane was Social. Four themes fell in the average range, including Artistic, Investigative, Conventional, and Realistic. Although the Social theme was moderately high, it was important to consider if the profile was relatively "flat" and, therefore, not very meaningful. In any case, this pattern in the profile suggested that she would find numerous occupations in the Occupational Scales with close to the same ratings in terms of similarity. This expectation was confirmed by the results of the SII. Such results suggested that Jane either was not mature enough, in terms of her self-awareness or knowledge about the world of work, to make a meaningful career decision, or that she valued variety. Some of the occupations that stood out for Jane were police officer, art teacher, musician, flight attendant, advertising executive, and special education teacher. Out of these occupations, the only one that Jane confirmed having an interest in was art teacher. She liked art, but had never given it consideration due to her perception that there were very few art-related jobs, and that those that were available generally paid poorly.

As the CDI was examined, it became apparent that Jane had not done much planning about her future career, and did not have the skills and awareness to make good decisions about her vocational future. These findings were of concern, especially due to her senior class status. She had found out where good sources of information were located, which was part of what had led her into counseling. Jane also had a low average awareness about jobs and what she needed to be successful. As a result of the CDI, counseling focused on raising her self-awareness, especially in relation to values, because such knowledge facilitates decision making.

The SI results were very consistent, with Study and Home/Family being highest across all three scales. Unlike many students, Jane's scores on Study and Work did not switch (Study becoming lower and Work becoming higher) as she progressed from the Participation scale to the Values Expectations scale. However, her Work score did get higher from Participation to the Values Expectations scale, and her Study score decreased with both being equal at the Values Expectations level. Her Commitment scale indicated that study was much more important to her than work. Jane had even stated that she wished she could stay in school and did not have to go to work.

The VS results tended to favor intrinsic over extrinsic values. Achievement, Ability Utilization, Creativity, and Personal Development were her top four rated values, all of which were intrinsic. Economic Security was her highest rated extrinsic value, and reflected part of her concern about remaining a journalism major. Intrinsic values tend to be reflective of occupations included in the Social and Artistic General Occupational Themes of the SII.

As Jane continued in counseling, the focus remained on raising her self-awareness and on learning to make decisions that reflected her values. The goal was to help her confirm herself by making decisions in line with what was important to her as an individual. Although the accuracy of the results was questioned due to the low scores on the Career Planning and Decision-Making scales of the CDI, the results of the SII remained relatively accurate. One perception was that Jane rejected many of the occupations that were rated similar for her on the Occupational Scales of the SII, accepting only art teacher as a possibility. This option seemed to be consistent with her interests, her preferred roles in life, and her values. Jane also was considering continuing her education by going to graduate school and studying either education or psychology, thus allowing her more time to make a decision before entering the world of work. This option was quite attractive to Jane; she had a high undergraduate grade point average, she would have had to take additional undergraduate hours to be eligible for a teaching certificate, and it would allow her to continue enhancing her career and educational development. At the time of termination, Jane was seeking admission to a graduate school in art education.

CONCLUSION

The preceding case studies have demonstrated the effectiveness of combining state-of-the-art assessment with the career counseling process, the essence of the C-DAC model. Each element of the C-DAC battery provides both comparative and confirmative data to supplement and enhance the counseling interview. The combination of counseling and assessment provides for powerful and meaningful interventions. There is no more appropriate time for using this model than during the typical college years, ages 18 to 23. The C-DAC model also is influential for individuals who are both younger and older because it provides numerous "pieces of the puzzle" that help individuals understand themselves and how each "piece" fits into all of life's activities, including work. Although incomplete in that the number of pieces that fit into this career development puzzle are difficult to count and even more difficult to assess, the C-DAC model provides an excellent means of completing this intricate puzzle. Through the utilization of the dynamic process suggested by this model, counselors can be of greater assistance in helping individuals make meaningful choices at each stage of development.

5

Donald E. Super's Theory and Career Development in Adulthood

Adults in today's society must be ready to cope with a world of work that is in a state of rapid transition. The emergence of new technologies often results in the creation of new occupational opportunities and the elimination of others. The trend toward corporate downsizing has forced many individuals to make job and occupational changes. The move from the industrial age to the information age has produced new workplace scenarios and options. These changes have caused many individuals to reevaluate their career goals and the meaning they derive from work (Maccoby, 1981; Savickas, 1993). As a result, many adults experience their career development as a continual process of making choices and adjusting to choices due to evolving self-concepts and occupational opportunities.

These fluctuations and evolutions in the nature of work result in a less than predictable process of career development for adults. The lack of an ontogenetic pattern of career development in adulthood has important theoretical implications, and points to some fundamental differences between adult and adolescent career development. For example, adults are engaged in the world of work, whereas adolescents are, at most, only engaged in work on a limited basis. Adolescents also have a time perspective toward work that is largely anticipatory (Super & Knasel, 1981). The type of awareness and information needed by adolescents is relatively universal. Adults, on the other hand, often need awareness and information that is particular to their individual career situations. Because of these differences, the career developmental tasks, the career development topics to be explored, and the kinds of occupational and self information needed by adults differ in comparison to adolescents. Super (1977) has pointed out that these differences lead to important distinctions in the meaning of the term "readiness for career decision making" when considering career development in adolescence versus career development in adulthood.

In discussing readiness for career decision making in adulthood, Super has used the term "career adaptability" (Super & Kidd, 1979; Super & Knasel, 1981). Although this term encompasses the same basic dimensions as the adolescent model of career maturity (i.e., planfulness, exploration, information, decision making, and reality orientation), the content and context of career decisions are different for adults when compared with adolescents. In acknowledgment of these differences, Super (1990) uses the term *career adaptability* because it reflects the necessity for being aware of the developmental tasks that one must cope with (both currently and in the near future). Of special importance here is the need for adults to develop "planfulness and foresight in looking and thinking ahead about one's work and working life" (Super et al., 1988a, p. 5). As noted earlier, the Adult Career Concerns Inventory (ACCI) has been developed in order to measure such attitudes. ACCI scores provide a structure for the consideration of the career developmental tasks about which individuals are concerned. Using Super's (1957) stage theory, we know that career development in adulthood typically involves the process of exploring occupational options, implementing career decisions, becoming established in a line of work, maintaining the occupational position attained, and preparing for retirement. Some (but increasingly fewer) individuals proceed through the tasks of the Exploration, Establishment, Maintenance, and Disengagement stages in a relatively linear fashion. Others experience a recycling through various tasks and stages. In other words, assuming that there is a relationship between one's chronological age and career developmental stage is risky. For example, a 21-year-old woman entering the workforce for the first time after graduating from college may find that the occupation she has chosen is not as satisfying as she had anticipated. Her lack of satisfaction may lead her to reevaluate her interests, skills, and values. After reconsidering these factors, she may opt for a new occupation and proceed to implement her new choice. A process such as this is an example of recycling from the Establishment stage to the Exploration stage tasks of crystallizing, specifying, and implementing a career choice. Or consider the 50-year-old man who has been "let go" from his long-term midlevel management position due to downsizing. Prior to proceeding with his job search, he may opt to engage in an intensive self-assessment process in which the decision is made to pursue a different occupational option. This process is an example of an individual who had been maintaining but then proceeded to recycle through Exploration stage tasks. It also is possible to be coping with the tasks of more than one career developmental stage at the same time. For instance, a woman in her late 40s who is attempting to hold onto her position within her occupational field also may be exploring other career options and considering retirement planning, all at the same time.

The ACCI can be used to relate the career concerns of clients to Super's career development stages and tasks. In this way, ACCI scores provide the counselor with a sense of direction as to what career development tasks should be the focal point for the counselor's career interventions. Also, by reviewing the career development stages within the ACCI, the counselor can teach the client about the process of career development in general. For example, the client's career can be reviewed in light of the career development stages and tasks the client has encountered. Self- and occupational insight can be increased by examining the manner in which the client coped with developmental tasks in the past. The client's future also can be discussed in terms of the career development tasks that are likely to be encountered. In this way, the client's understanding of time perspective and planfulness can be enhanced.

The use of the ACCI and the term career adaptability also provide counselors with the opportunity to explore with the client the distinctions between the "maxicycle" of one's career and the "minicycles" that individuals experience at the transition points between career stages (Super, 1980). More specifically, when considering the *maxicycle* of one's career, the concern is with relating career developmental tasks to the five major life stages (i.e., Growth, Exploration, Establishment, Maintenance, and Disengagement). The ACCI is useful in helping clients understand how their career concerns relate to the maxicycle of career development.

On the other hand, the term *minicycle* has to do with describing the Growth, Exploration, Establishment, Maintenance, and Disengagement experienced at the transition points from one maxicycle stage to the next, that is, "whenever careers become unstabilized, leading to new growth, reexploration, and reestablishment (Herr & Cramer, 1992, p. 214). For example, upon beginning a new job the college graduate may go through a period of growth in the new role, exploration of the expectations and requirements within the role, become established in the role as a result of an increase in competence, experience maintenance in the role if it has been satisfying and performance has been acceptable, and experience disengagement if interest in the role declines, and, as a result of further growth, other occupational options become more attractive (Super, 1990).

Of course, the decisions adults make about occupational options— that is, which to pursue, which to eliminate from consideration, etc.— are complex. They involve a myriad of determinants. In Super's (1990) Archway Model (see Figure 1.2), he attempts to identify the personal (e.g., values, needs, interests) and situational (e.g., community, economy, society, labor market) determinants of career development. In identifying these determinants, Super (1980) has noted:

> The decision points of a life career reflect encounters with a variety of personal and situational determinants. The former consist of the genetic constitution of the individual modified by his or her experiences (the environment and its situational determinants) in the womb, in the home, and in the community. The latter are the geographic, historic, social, and economic conditions in which the individual functions from infancy through adulthood and old age. (p. 294)

The interactions among these various determinants serve to influence the career developmental stage of the individuals as well as the individual's role self-concepts. Role self-concepts are especially important to consider in the career development of adults.

Super (1980) has addressed the importance of role self-concepts within the context of his Life-Career Rainbow (see Figure 1.3). Noting that "a career is defined as the combination and sequence of roles played by a person during the course of a lifetime" (Super, 1980, p. 282), Super has identified nine major roles and four principal theaters in which the roles are played. It is the interaction of personal and situational determinants that influence the degree of salience any role holds for the individual. Salience, in this instance, refers to the attitudinal, cognitive, and behavioral dimensions of the relative importance of any life role (Super, 1980).

The Life-Career Rainbow model is an effective vehicle for helping adults understand the relative importance of the various life roles in their lives. Super (1984) has pointed out that the "failure to take this multiplicity and interaction of life career roles into account has been, and to a degree still is, one of the most serious shortcomings of educational and vocational guidance" (p. 34). By using the Life-Career Rainbow, counselors can explore ways in which the life roles of their clients interact and what changes, if any, clients may choose to make in their life role participation.

The Life-Career Rainbow also can be used to enhance the time perspective of clients. That is, in reviewing what their life role participation has been and what it is now, clients can discuss the degree of satisfaction they have experienced in their life roles. Counselors can accomplish this by using the figure of the rainbow. More specifically, clients can portray their participation by coloring in the appropriate bands with each band representing a specific life role. The amount of participation can be represented by varying the band width for each life role; that is, a wider band equals more participation. As Super (1980) has suggested, the intensity of participation in each life role can be represented by the degree of shading used within each band (e.g., dark green to represent the role of child as primary, dark purple to portray the primacy of the spousal role, or light red to represent a reluctant student).

Counselors also can use The Salience Inventory (SI) (Nevill & Super, 1986c) as a tool for exploring the life role participation and commitment of their clients. By focusing on the degree of agreement between the Participation and Commitment subscales, the counselor and client can explore issues such as role conflict, role balance, and time management. For example, the client who has an average score of 3.9 (out of a possible 4.0) on the Commitment to Home and Family scale and a score of 1.9 on the Participation in Home and Family scale can be encouraged to discuss this discrepancy. Perhaps the client's commitment to Home and Family is not as strong as the client reported. On the other hand, it may be that the client is experiencing time pressure due to activities related to the worker role. Super (1980) has suggested that "success in one role facilitates success in others, and difficulties in one role are likely to lead to difficulties in another" (p. 287). With this in mind, if the commitment score of 3.9 for the client mentioned above is accurate, then the counselor can help the client to understand the importance of committing more time to the role of home and family. In this instance, time management training could lead to the realization that it is possible, with good planning, to spend more time at home and not experience a decline in work performance.

The Values Expectations subscale of the SI also is very useful in helping adults understand the values they expect to be able to express in life roles. Super (1957, 1990) has illustrated the benefits of exploring life role participation in his discussion of the cases of John Stasko and J.C., respectively. Whether using the rainbow figure or the SI, counselors can help their clients make plans for what they would like their life role participation to be in the future in order to enhance their career satisfaction. It is important to note that the counselor also can encourage the client to take The Values Scale (VS) (Nevill & Super, 1989a) in order to extend the number of values the client is examining. Such exploration can help clients understand the meaning they seek in their life role participation.

When used in these ways, Super's concepts and assessment instruments help adult career counseling clients to understand the personal constructs that they use to make sense out of the personal and situational determinants that have shaped and are shaping their career development.

C-DAC INSTRUMENTS AND WORK IMPORTANCE STUDY RESEARCH

The trends of increased sensitivity to multiculturalism, of corporate downsizing, the explosion of information, and the increased frequency of career change are transforming the perspectives of career counselors and the goals of career counseling clients (Savickas, 1993). Many career counseling clients today are seeking assistance not only in making occupational choices, but they also are concerned about increasing the sense of meaningfulness they experience in their lives. They are evaluating how they are spending their time, what they are committed to, and what is important to them (Anderson & Niles, 1995). As clients focus more directly on these topics of concern, counselors must respond with appropriate career interventions. The Work Importance Study (WIS) has provided the career counseling field with important information for facilitating the career development process in the postmodern era.

The results of much of the WIS research indicate that, across the life span, the consideration of life role salience and values is critical for increasing understanding relative to how people and their careers develop. These research findings are providing important information concerning the relationship among career salience, values, and other important career development constructs (e.g., career self-efficacy, self-esteem, and developmental task achievement). In order to examine these research findings more closely, attention is now focused on selected findings from the WIS research as they relate to career development in adulthood.

In a study that examined the relations among age, role salience, and career maturity in a group of 281 community college students, Helms (1991) found that study participants with higher scores on the Establishment Scale of the ACCI also had higher scores on the Commitment to Work scale of the SI. Study participants with higher scores on the Exploration scale of the ACCI also had higher scores on the Commitment to Study scale of the SI. This finding makes sense from a developmental perspective in that one would expect individuals who are concerned with tasks of the establishment stage to be more committed to work than individuals who are still occupationally undecided.

A study conducted by Veeder (1991) examined the differences in scores on the SI using a sample of women enrolled in MBA programs in two universities in the northeast, and graduates of those programs who had worked in the last 2 years. There were significant differences between the younger and older groups in participation and values expectations for the role of worker and for participation in the role of home and family. More specifically, in terms of the work role, there was a significantly lower score in values expectations around work for the older women compared with the younger group. The younger group anticipated conflict in personal and professional integration in the next 5 years as they approach the Age Thirty Transition.

In a study of the differences in life satisfaction, work satisfaction, and role salience between executive women (ages 35 to 55) who changed careers at midlife and those who did not, it was found that "persisters" scored higher in commitment to work than "changers" (Pope, 1989). Both persisters and changers increased their commitment to leisure across time, and the work role was the most salient for the persisters and changers; the homemaker role was a close second. Persisters and changers differed on only two areas in values expectations. Persisters expected to help people with problems in work more than changers; persisters also expected that they could live life their own way in the home more than changers. No other differences were found in 14 values around work and home.

Yates (1990b) investigated the VS's construct validity through a comparison of scores on the 21 scales of the VS across four age groups and five occupational groups. The following age groups were created using cutoffs derived from Super's (1957) developmental theory and views of midlife transition periods from Murphy and Burck (1976): (a) 18 to 25 years, (b) 26 to 35 years, (c) 36 to 45 years, and (d) 46 to 62 years. Occupational groups were created using Holland's (1973) theory. The results of the discriminant analysis suggested that 18 to 25 year olds placed relatively more emphasis on physical activity, advancement, and social interaction, and less emphasis on autonomy and working conditions. These findings are logical and supportive of the construct validity of the VS.

With respect to the occupational groups in the Yates (1990a) study, persons in Realistic occupations placed more value on physical prowess and risk than other Holland categories. Persons in Conventional or Enterprising occupations emphasized the values of working conditions and economic security. Overall, Yates concluded that the results supported the conclusion that the VS is a useful measure for counselors interested in assessing the values of adult clients.

Torres (1991) examined the relationship between work values and job satisfaction in a group of African American and Hispanic candidates for the Minority Leadership Development Project at Texas A & M University. More specifically, Torres used scores from the VS and the Minnesota Importance Questionnaire to predict job satisfaction. Results from regression analyses indicated that four VS variables (Autonomy, Personal Development, Social Relations, and Variety) and one variable from the Minnesota Importance Questionnaire (Company Policies and Practices) were significant predictors of job satisfaction for this sample.

Bartley (1989) investigated the effects of a prison vocational education training program on the work values of mentally retarded inmates and also compared values scores between the mentally retarded prisoners participating in his study and the normative sample scores provided in the VS manual. Findings of Bartley's study suggested that the vocational training program resulted in significant increases in scores on the values of altruism, risk, and physical prowess. Bartley also found significant differences between the adult norm sample and the mentally retarded prison sample on the values of ability utilization, achievement, aesthetics, altruism, autonomy, personal development, physical activity, risk, working conditions, cultural identity, and physical prowess.

Although this review of the WIS research using adults as study participants is not exhaustive, it does provide the reader with a sense of the ways in which scores from the VS and the SI are providing important information relative to the career development of adults. From these studies we are learning more about the nature of career salience for different groups of individuals, as well as what members of diverse populations and different occupational groups value. Acquiring more information about what life roles are important to people and what they value is critical to the career counseling process.

USING THE C-DAC MODEL TO UNDERSTAND ADULT CAREER COUNSELING CLIENTS

The application of the C-DAC model is discussed using a specific counseling center as a backdrop. At the University of Virginia, adult clients are seen for career counseling in the Personal and Career Development Center (PCDC). Clients in the PCDC are on average, female, approximately 35 years old, married or recently divorced, Caucasian, and relatively highly educated (mean years in school = 15.4, SD = 2.3). PCDC services are available at no charge to adults not enrolled at the University of Virginia. Counseling services in the PCDC are provided by advanced master's and doctoral degree students enrolled in the counselor education program at the University of Virginia. Counselors are trained in the C-DAC model and are supervised by counselor education faculty members. The average counseling relationship lasts for approximately eight sessions (SD = 2.4).

All clients in the PCDC complete, at intake, an assessment battery that includes the ACCI, the VS, the SI, and the Occupational Stress Inventory (OSI; Osipow & Spokane, 1987). Typically, clients complete the assessments prior to their first counseling sessions.

RESULTS OF ACCI, OSI, VS, AND SI SCORES FOR PCDC CLIENTS

As a beginning step in understanding what adult career counseling clients "look like," it is useful to examine the average scores for clients from the PCDC. In order to accomplish this, raw scores and T-scores from the ACCI, OSI, VS, and SI for a sample of PCDC clients are provided and then discussed. Reporting the scores in this way allows the reader to understand how PCDC clients tend to respond to the items on the various inventories and also provides a comparison between PCDC clients' scores and scores from the adult norm groups provided in the respective inventory manuals.

Table 5.1 provides information concerning the means and standard deviations for stage scores on the ACCI. Both male and female PCDC clients tend to have career concerns related to the Exploration stage. These clients, therefore, tend to be most concerned with clarifying their ideas about the type of work they would like to do and making a choice among the occupations they are considering. The pattern of scores on the ACCI is essentially the same for males and females. The level of concern for Exploration stage tasks is significantly higher for male and female PCDC clients when they are compared with adults in general (see Figure 5.1). PCDC clients have Exploration stage scores that are approximately one standard deviation above the norm. This pattern of scores for the ACCI is not surprising given that PCDC clients are career counseling clients. Given the additional life issues that often confront adults in career transition, adults who are considering significant career changes also may be

TABLE 5.1 Adult Career Concerns Inventory Average Client Scores

	Males		Females	
	M	SD	M	SD
Exploration	3.93	.69	4.13	.65
Crystallization	4.06	.72	4.19	.79
Specification	4.07	.71	4.20	.67
Implementation	3.87	.84	3.99	.78
Establishment	3.27	.83	3.23	.79
Stabilization	3.34	.98	3.30	.91
Consolidation	3.35	.88	3.19	.94
Advancement	3.16	1.06	3.21	1.03
Maintenance	3.16	.86	3.23	.85
Holding	2.81	.81	2.90	1.01
Updating	3.08	1.06	3.22	1.05
Innovating	3.49	.97	3.48	.97
Disengagement	2.86	.88	2.89	.82
Deceleration	3.04	1.07	2.64	.87
Retirement Planning	2.81	1.04	2.89	1.07
Retirement Living	2.77	.91	2.53	.91

FIGURE 5.1 ACCI T-Scores: Average Client

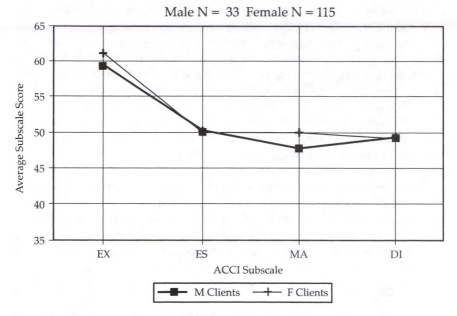

Note: EX = Exploration; ES = Establishment; MA = Maintenance; DI = Disengagement.

experiencing stress and strain. Because of this possibility, it is useful to examine scores on the OSI.

In general, the OSI scores for clients in the PCDC (see Table 5.2) indicate that male clients tend to experience high levels of occupational stress in the form of role insufficiency (i.e., a poor fit between their skills and the job they are performing) and high levels of strain in the form of vocational strain (i.e., having poor attitudes toward work, including dread and apathy to their physical health). Female PCDC clients' scores differ substantially from male clients' scores. Whereas female clients reported average scores for occupational stress, strain, and coping, men reported higher stress and strain scores and lower coping scores. This suggests that male adult career counseling clients may be more "at risk" for experiencing personal adjustment and career adjustment issues. This point is made more dramatically in Figure 5.2. Here T-scores are used to compare male and female career counseling client scores to males and females in the normative sample. Although scores for the female clients are slightly beyond one-half of a standard deviation from the mean (i.e., role insufficiency and psychological strain), males have eleven OSI T-scores that are significantly different from the mean T-score of 50.

TABLE 5.2 Occupational Stress Inventory Average Client Scores

Subscale	Men		Women	
	M	SD	M	SD
RO	24.6	7.7	23.3	6.8
RI	34.9	5.8	31.3	8.7
RA	24.8	7.2	21.3	6.1
RB	25.6	6.5	23.5	7.3
R	23.8	7.3	21.4	6.5
PE	19.4	7.1	15.0	4.8
VS	24.4	5.5	20.0	5.4
PSY	27.9	9.0	24.7	8.2
IS	23.6	7.3	21.8	5.7
PHS	23.1	7.9	20.8	7.4
RE	24.1	5.7	26.5	5.9
SC	26.1	4.6	28.5	6.6
SS	37.4	7.4	39.8	7.3
RC	32.6	8.1	36.0	5.5

Note: RO = Role Overload; RI = Role Insufficiency; RA = Role Ambiguity; RB = Role Boundary; R = Responsibility; PE = Physical Environment; VS = Vocational Strain; PSY = Psychological Strain; IS = Interpersonal Strain; PHS = Physical Strain; RE = Recreation; SC = Social Contact; SS = Social Support; RC = Rational Cognitive.

There are numerous hypotheses one can generate about these OSI scores. For instance, gender differences in OSI scores may be due to a cultural socialization process that results in men being more resistant to seeking counseling help. Higher male scores on the OSI may, therefore, reflect the higher stress and strain threshold necessary to cause male clients to seek counseling. Career counselors working with adult male clients may find it useful to be cognizant of the potential for these clients to have extreme OSI scores and to expand their treatment interventions to address their clients' specific issues related to occupational stress and strain. In this regard, the extended report form provided by the test publisher is extremely useful in providing possible treatment strategies.

It is useful to look at scores on the VS in order to determine (a) whether there are gender differences related to values and (b) whether there is a pattern to the values PCDC clients seek to express in their activities and life roles. Table 5.3 consists of means and standard deviations for the raw scores for male and female PCDC clients. Essentially, there are no differences between males and females on these scores (although some statistically significant differences exist, these differences are of such magnitude that they are of no clinical significance). The raw scores indicate

FIGURE 5.2   OSI T-Scores: Average Client

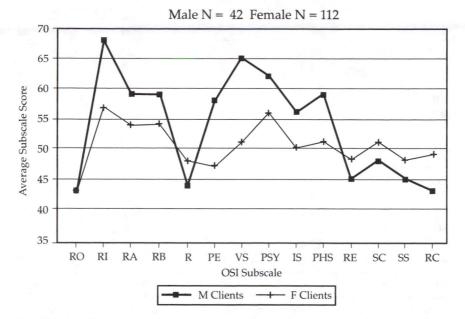

Note: RO = Role Overload; RI = Role Insufficiency; RA = Role Ambiguity; RB = Role Boundary; R = Responsibility; PE = Physical Environment; VS = Vocational Strain; PSY = Psychological Strain; IS = Interpersonal Strain; PHS = Physical Strain; RE = Recreation; SC = Social Contact; SS = Social Support; RC = Rational Cognitive.

that PCDC clients tend to view ability utilization, achievement, altruism, economic rewards, lifestyle, personal development, working conditions, and economic security as important values (i.e., raw scores >15). Common sense suggests that these are not surprising given that they are drawn from a sample of adults who have voluntarily sought career counseling. That is, when an adult who seeks to express the values of personal development and ability utilization experiences a job situation that is not allowing for the expression of these values, career counseling is an appropriate place to turn for assistance. In using T-scores to compare male and female PCDC clients to samples provided in the VS manual (see Figure 5.3), it is apparent that male clients are different from males in the normative sample in that they tend to place a higher value on aesthetics, personal development, and economic security than males in the norm group.

It is interesting to note that males and females who are clients in the PCDC tend to place greater importance on the value of personal development than the males and females in the normative groups. This

TABLE 5.3   The Values Scale Means and Standard Deviations

	Males		Females	
	M	SD	M	SD
Abu	16.90	2.09	17.00	2.11
Ach	17.10	2.08	17.60	2.10
Adv	13.20	3.65	13.21	3.66
Aes	14.01	3.89	14.17	3.75
Alt	14.45	3.39	15.11	3.31
Ath	11.75	3.17	11.24	3.21
Aut	14.65	2.60	15.00	2.91
Cre	14.54	3.41	14.51	3.39
Ecr	14.80	3.41	14.80	3.40
Lis	15.85	2.28	15.82	2.29
Ped	17.27	2.15	17.41	2.14
Pha	11.76	3.28	11.25	3.27
Pre	13.78	3.31	14.00	3.45
Ris	8.51	2.82	8.53	2.84
Soi	12.32	2.95	12.33	2.94
Sor	14.27	2.78	14.36	2.76
Var	13.35	3.01	14.01	3.35
Woc	14.92	2.45	15.35	2.74
Cui	11.79	3.53	11.87	3.55
Php	7.11	2.11	7.13	2.21
Ecs	16.99	2.97	16.13	2.83

Note: Abu = Ability Utilization; Ach = Achievement; Adv = Advancement; Aes = Aesthetics; Alt = Altruism; Ath = Authority; Aut = Autonomy; Cre = Creativity; Ecr = Economic Rewards; Lis = Life Style; Ped = Personal Development; Pha = Physical Activity; Pre = Prestige; Ris = Risk; Soi = Social Interaction; Sor = Social Relations; Var = Variety; Woc = Working Conditions; Cui = Cultural Identity; Php = Physical Prowess; Ecs = Economic Security.

characteristic naturally leads to some speculation. For example, is this value (i.e., personal development) an important variable in leading individuals who are in unfavorable work situations to seek career counseling? Or is it that being in a work situation where one experiences role insufficiency leads to placing a higher importance on the value of personal development? Although the answers to these questions are beyond the scope of the data that have been collected thus far, these are interesting and important questions for understanding career development in adulthood.

The scores from SI also reveal interesting information concerning the life role importance of clients and the values they expect to be able to express in the major life roles. Table 5.4 contains the means and standard

FIGURE 5.3   VS T-Scores: Average Client

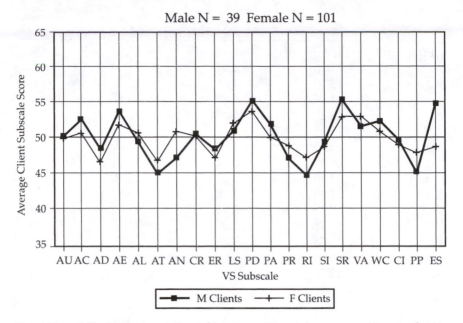

Male N = 39 Female N = 101

Note: AU = Ability Utilization; AC = Achievement; AD = Advancement; AE = Aesthetics; AL = Altruism; AT = Authority; AN = Autonomy; CR = Creativity; ER = Economic Rewards; LS = Life Style; PD = Personal Development; PA = Physical Activity; PR = Prestige; RI = Risk; SI = Social Interaction; SR = Social Relations; VA = Variety; WC = Working Conditions; CI = Cultural Identity; PP = Physical Prowess; ES = Economic Security.

deviations for PCDC client scores on the SI. Given that the response options for the SI range from a low of 1 ("never") to a high of 4 ("always"), it is interesting to note that the PCDC clients have relatively low participation scores in all life roles measured by the SI. In comparison, commitment scores are higher with the Commitment to Work, Commitment to Home and Family, and Commitment to Leisure scores all being greater than 3.0. The only score on the Values Expectation scale that is 3.0 or greater is the score related to home and family (although the values expectations score for the worker role approaches 3.0). Given these scores, one can wonder as to the motivation and enthusiasm PCDC clients possess when it comes to considering their life role participation. If PCDC clients do not expect to be able to express important values in the major life roles, then they may not be willing to commit the time and energy to the career counseling process that is necessary for effective career decision making. In these instances counselors may need to encourage clients to examine

TABLE 5.4 The Salience Inventory Means and Standard Deviations

	Males		Females	
	M	SD	M	SD
Participation				
Study	21.21	6.90	21.71	6.90
Work	26.89	5.06	28.16	5.04
Community Service	17.76	6.99	18.08	6.02
Home/Family	24.73	5.90	27.86	4.89
Leisure	25.79	5.70	26.07	5.31
Commitment				
Study	26.72	7.82	27.11	7.23
Work	30.97	4.32	31.97	4.93
Community Service	25.00	8.23	25.72	6.42
Home/Family	32.79	6.99	35.67	4.72
Leisure	3.06	6.83	31.17	6.19
Value Expectations				
Study	33.03	9.13	32.82	8.97
Work	40.18	7.62	40.94	7.59
Community Service	29.45	9.81	32.71	8.49
Home/Family	39.12	7.26	43.03	7.83
Leisure	39.36	8.36	40.04	7.79

their career beliefs (Krumboltz, 1988). For instance, it may be that lower values expectations scores are a reflection of previous and/or current unsatisfying work situations. What has been, or what is, does not always have to translate into what will be. Through appropriate self-assessment and occupational exploration, some clients will be able to obtain jobs that offer more opportunities for values expression. Communicating this to clients may help to increase their hopefulness for having opportunities to express key values within their life roles.

There are several differences that are noteworthy when comparing PCDC client scores on the SI to scores for males and females in the norm group (see Figure 5.4). Female PCDC clients tend to score lower on the Participation in Study, Participation in Work, Commitment to Work, Commitment to Leisure, Values Expectations for Study, Values Expectations for Work, and Values Expectations for Home and Family scales when compared with females in the normative sample. The remainder of the female PCDC clients' scores are similar to the scores for females in the norm group. Male PCDC clients score higher than males in the norm

FIGURE 5.4 SI T-Scores: Average Client

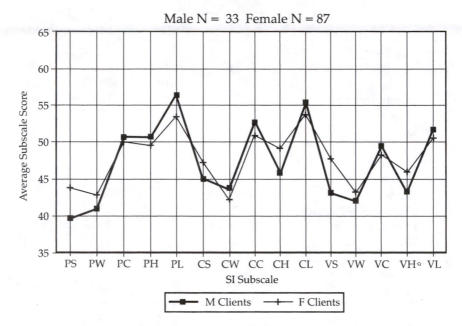

Note: P = Participation; S = Study; W = Work; C = Community Service; H = Home/ Family; L = Leisure; C = Commitment; V = Value Expectations.

group on the Participation in Leisure and Commitment to Leisure scales. Male PCDC clients also score lower than males in the norm group on the Participation in Study, Participation in Work, Commitment to Work, Values Expectations for Study, Values Expectations for Work, and Values Expectations for Home and Family scales.

For both males and females who are clients in the PCDC, the leisure role is important. Nothing is known about the specific reason why PCDC clients see this role as being so salient, but one can speculate that their participation and commitment is either complementary or supplementary to their participation in the role of worker. Exploring the nature of the low Commitment to Work scores for males and females also is a worthwhile counseling and research task. For instance, it is worth exploring whether this score is more state or trait related. In essence, reviewing these scores is a useful exercise in helping counselors and researchers to generate hypotheses about the general nature of adult career counseling clients. But, because the assessment scores that have been discussed are averages, they may or may not apply to the individual client. Given this fact, it is helpful to consider ways in which the C-DAC model can be used in providing career counseling to adult clients.

USING THE C-DAC MODEL WITH ADULT CAREER COUNSELING CLIENTS

The implementation of the C-DAC model in career counseling with adults can occur in several ways or sequences (Niles & Usher, 1993; Super et al., 1992). Although there are exceptions, the most typical sequence at the University of Virginia is as follows: (1) ACCI, (2) OSI, (3) SII, (4) VS, (5) SI.

The ACCI results are examined before the initial counseling session in order to gain a sense of the client's career concerns in relation to the maxicycle stages and tasks. That is, the ACCI results provide an indication as to whether the client is concerned with career exploration, establishment, maintenance, and/or disengagement. The counselor also examines the OSI prior to meeting with the client. This is done in order to gain an understanding of the degree to which the client is experiencing occupational stress and personal strain (Osipow & Spokane, 1987). By examining OSI scores, the counselor also can gain an understanding of the coping resources used by the client.

Focusing on the ACCI and OSI prior to the initial counseling session provides useful (albeit tentative) information as to the client's readiness for focusing on career decision making. For example, a client with OSI results that reveal high scores on the Psychological Strain scale (indicating depression) and low scores on the Social Support and Self-Care scales might need to focus on increasing coping resources prior to addressing career concerns. In addition to self-care issues (e.g., sleep, eating, exercise), typical counseling strategies in this instance might include encouraging the client to consider joining a support group or a group related to a vocational interest area. A client with high Vocational Strain scores (suggesting feelings of dread, boredom, and disinterest toward work) and considerable concern for the career developmental tasks of the Exploration stage may need opportunities to express the strong emotions being experienced as a result of an unfavorable work situation prior to focusing on the task of crystallization.

Similarly, a client with OSI scores indicating a high level of vocational strain and poor rational-cognitive coping resources may lack a sense of hopefulness about the career-planning process or lack the problem-solving skills required to accurately translate self-assessment data into a career choice (i.e., to complete the task of the Exploration stage). In this instance, the counselor may find it useful to teach basic career planning concepts and problem-solving skills as part of the career intervention.

Once the client's concerns for the various career developmental tasks have been identified and the client's stress, strain, and coping resources have been addressed, the counseling process typically moves on to con-

129

sider the client's interests, values, and life role salience (Super, 1990; Super et al., 1992). Inventory results are examined in light of both their public/objective meaning and their private/subjective meaning (Savickas, 1993). These interpretation strategies relate to Super's (1990) notion that "self-concept theory might better be called personal construct theory, to show the individual's dual focus on self and on situation" (p. 222). That is, scores are reported to clients in terms of what they mean in a normative sense and scores are used to help clients explore the personal meaning they attach to them. For example, a client can be encouraged to discuss the specific ways in which the value of personal development is expressed in the life roles of worker and leisurite. Or a client can be encouraged to provide a more specific definition for the value of economic security. The client who obtains a high score on the Responsibility subscale of the OSI can be queried as to why it is preferable to "be in charge" as opposed to "following orders." This type of questioning can be used to begin a process of "laddering" (Cochran, 1992) in order to uncover the personal constructs the client attaches to values, interests, and life role participation.

In order to provide a more specific example of the application of the C-DAC model in career counseling with adults, three counseling cases from the PCDC are presented and discussed.

THE CASE OF DONALD

Donald, a 40-year-old Caucasian male, entered counseling in the spring of 1993. Despite the fact that he possessed a bachelor's degree in architecture and a master's degree in landscape architecture, Donald had been unemployed for a period of 1 year when he entered career counseling. During his intake interview, Donald mentioned feeling dissatisfied with his previous jobs. Most recently, he had been employed as a landscape architect and reported enjoying the creative aspects of his work. He also said, however, that he had experienced difficulty in getting along with his supervisor and that this was a pattern for him in his previous employment situations. He further reported a strong dislike for structured work environments. He related that he experienced a high level of anxiety when confronted with challenging tasks. Donald also noted that he was typically very sensitive to criticism. His hobbies included photography, work with computers, and reading in the areas of human potential, spirituality, and psychology.

An additional factor concerning Donald's situation at the time he entered counseling was that he and his wife were in the process of divorcing. The divorce proceedings were focused on the issues of child support and custody relative to Donald's 4-year-old son. Donald's father was employed as an engineer and his mother was a clinical psychologist (both were retired). Donald was their only child. In the course of counseling, Donald related that he felt that he never received from his parents "what he needed." He perceived both parents as being somewhat distant and his father as being rather critical. Both parents were anxious for him to return to work.

Donald's C-DAC Results

Occupational Stress Inventory

  (Reported in T-Scores)

  Occupational Roles Questionnaire:
    Role Overload 40
    Role Insufficiency 80
    Role Ambiguity 66
    Role Boundary 70
    Responsibility 44
    Physical Environment 43

  Personal Strain Questionnaire:
    Vocational Strain 78
    Psychological Strain 77
    Interpersonal Strain 78
    Physical Strain 74

  Personal Resources Questionnaire:
    Recreation 47
    Self-care 58
    Social Support 38
    Rational/Cognitive Coping 24

Strong Interest Inventory
    Academic Comfort: 44
    Introversion-Extroversion: 68

  Themes:
    Realistic .... Average 52
    Artistic .... Mod. High 51
    Investigative .... Average 40
    Conventional .... Mod. Low 40
    Social .... Low 37
    Enterprising .... Low 37

  Basic Interest
    High: .... Art 61
    Mod. High: .... Writing 54
                                Teaching 59

(continued)

Occupations:
  Investigative:
      Computer Programmer 49
      Geographer 45
      College Professor 50
      Psychologist 48
  Artistic:
      Artist, Fine 47
      Artist, Commercial 46
      Architect 52
      Photography 55
      Musician 49
      Advertising Executive 46
      Librarian 47

The Values Scale:
  (Ratings Range from 1 = Low to 4 = High)
    4.0 .... Aesthetics
    4.0 .... Autonomy
    4.0 .... Creativity
    4.0 .... Prestige
    3.8 .... Personal Development
    3.6 .... Achievement
    3.6 .... Economic Rewards
    3.6 .... Working Conditions
    3.0 .... Ability Utilization
    3.0 .... Authority
    3.0 .... Life Style
    2.8 .... Economic Security
    2.6 .... Altruism
    2.6 .... Physical Activity
    2.4 .... Advancement
    2.2 .... Social Relations
    1.6 .... Risk
    1.4 .... Social Interaction
    1.4 .... Cultural Identity
    1.2 .... Variety
    1.0 .... Physical Prowess

Adult Career Concerns Inventory
  Number of concerns rated 4 or 5 (considerable or great)
  Exploration Stage
      Crystallization 4
      Specification 3
      Implementation 2
      Total 9

(continued)

Establishment Stage
Stabilizing 0
Consolidating 2
Advancing 2
Total 4

Maintenance Stage
Holding 0
Updating 4
Innovation 4
Total 8

Disengagement Stage
Decelerating 0
Retirement Plan 0
Retirement Living 1
Total 1

The Salience Inventory

(Ratings Range from 1 = Low to 4 = High)

	Study	Work	Community Service	Home & Family	Leisure Activities
Participation	3.6	2.6	1.5	2.7	2.4
Commitment	3.8	3.0	2.0	3.9	3.3
Values Expectations	2.9	2.0	1.4	2.4	2.4

Using the C-DAC Battery With Donald

The results of the Occupational Roles Questionnaire of the Occupational Stress Inventory indicated that Donald experienced his work environment as disorganized and unstructured (high scores on the Role Insufficiency, Role Ambiguity, and Role Boundary subscales).

Examination of his Personal Strain scores suggested that Donald was experiencing emotional and physical symptoms of distress, including a high degree of boredom and disinterest related to work, feelings of depression and/or irritability, impaired interpersonal relationships, and doubt about work performance. The pattern of scores obtained by Donald suggests that he had little relief from psychological strain at work, home, or in the social environment.

Exacerbating the problems reflected in these scores was the low level of coping resources demonstrated on the Personal Resources Questionnaire, especially in regard to Social Support and Rational/Cognitive Coping. These low scores suggested that Donald felt isolated and that he did not have access to people he "could count on" for support. In addition, these scores suggested a deficiency in cognitive coping skills and problem-solving skills.

Given these scores, it is not surprising that Donald evidenced a high degree of faulty thinking in the initial stages of counseling. More specifically, Donald often engaged in "all-or-nothing" thinking, which was demonstrated by a tendency to evaluate his personal qualities in extreme, black-or-white categories. All-or-nothing thinking forms the basis for perfectionism. In Donald's case it caused him to interpret any mistake or deficiency (no matter how slight) as proof of his worthlessness and inadequateness. By forcing his self-evaluations into absolute categories (either he was a "100" or a "0") he set himself up to be constantly depressed. It is not surprising, therefore, that he frequently engaged in discrediting his skills and experiences because they never measured up to his exaggerated expectations. Often this self-perceived "incompetency" was used as a rationale for not pursuing career-related options.

Much of the first months of counseling with Donald focused on his tendency to engage in all-or-nothing thinking and an exaggerated desire to receive affirmation from others. Counseling related to the latter issue focused on his tendency to act "like a chameleon." That is, in new social situations he would observe interactions and try to interpret the norms and expectations of others in these scenarios. He would then try to behave in ways that would elicit approval from others—discounting his own sense of who he was and what was important to him. This pattern led to a general sense of identity confusion and complicated the process of self-assessment related to career decision making.

Exploration of this issue then led to focusing on his underlying sense of not feeling "OK" about himself. A significant influence in this regard was Donald's perception of his father as being overly critical. We explored the effects of this for Donald and ways in which he may have been perpetuating negative self-beliefs related to childhood interactions with his father. Much of the latter exploration focused on Donald's need to learn how to be more nurturing—to himself and to others. We also examined his reluctance to trust his own sense of who he was and what he wanted for himself in his life and work.

Interspersed throughout counseling, Donald had mentioned interests and activities that were important to him. We spent a significant amount of time clarifying the interests, skills, and values he identified as being important. Still, he was cautious about trusting his judgment in this regard. The assessment results, therefore, provided him with an opportunity to "reality check" the variables he had identified as being important for his career decision making.

The results of the ACCI reflected concern with clarifying ideas about the type of work Donald would enjoy doing. Additionally, Donald's scores suggested considerable concern with updating his knowledge and skills in his field and learning new skills to improve his work performance.

Donald's scores on the SII provided an indication of interest areas that were important for him to consider in his career decision making. Throughout his counseling, Donald had identified an interest in engaging in creative activities, especially in the areas of photography and computer design. He also had referred to the fact that he disliked structured environments. (He felt these to be confining and restricting.) It was important for Donald to receive the feedback from his SII scores that he was, in fact, an Artistic type in Holland's scheme of things. He evidenced high interests in artistic activities and reported interests that were similar to individuals in a variety of artistic occupations. Donald also achieved consistent scores by demonstrating similar interests with individuals in Investigative occupations, such as computer programmer and college professor. This preference toward working with data and things, rather than people, also was supported by his score on the Introversion-Extroversion scale (68).

Donald's scores on the VS also confirmed his artistic bent, as creativity and aesthetics were strong values for him. It also was true that autonomy was a highly prized value. In this regard, it is interesting to note that Donald had spoken of a desire to be in an occupation that allowed him to establish his own hours and be his own boss. In this way, the VS provided him with useful feedback concerning the validity of these goals.

Donald felt that his scores for the values of Prestige and Personal Development (4.0 and 3.8, respectively) reflected his need to feel "OK" about himself, and for others to respect him and his work.

The final assessment instrument reviewed with Donald was the SI. Scores on this assessment indicated that Donald spent much of his time participating in studying, with less time spent in the areas of home and family, work, leisure activities, and community activities. These results were of interest in light of his scores on the Commitment scale. Specifically, Donald felt a high level of commitment to the roles of home and family and studying. Although the participation and commitment scores for studying were consistent (3.6 and 3.8, respectively), the participation and commitment scores for home and family (2.7 and 3.9, respectively) were fairly discrepant, suggesting that this role was a greater priority on an affective level than behaviorally. In counseling with Donald, it was apparent that his pending divorce and the associated custody issues were contributing to this discrepancy in significant ways. He was spending less time with his son and although he was pursuing custody, the outcome of this issue was in doubt. Donald also reported that his home environment was tremendously important to him. For example, it was important for him to decorate his home in a way that reflected who he was. This was, in essence, another form of creative self-expression for him. In this regard, he noted that since relocating to his new apartment he had not really attended to the details necessary to make his new living quarters feel like home.

Lastly, the scores on the Values Expectations scales of the SI reflected low expectations for all roles. Donald seemed to feel some degree of hopelessness for realizing his values through any life roles. These scores are not surprising, given the fact that Donald noted a feeling of depression at the time he entered career counseling. The scores on the Values Expectations scale were, therefore, examined in light of earlier counseling issues pertaining to the difference in pursuing activities because they were meaningful and interesting to him rather than acting according to an external set of standards and expectations.

The net effect of reviewing the scores from the C-DAC instruments was that Donald felt more confident with regard to his thinking about his career direction. Exploration of values and role salience issues helped him to verify and validate what things were of importance to him. As he processed these variables against the backdrop of previous counseling issues, he seemed to be giving himself permission to risk behaving in ways that were congruent with his values and interests. The process of incorporating personal and career issues in this way was an affirming and empowering process for Donald.

THE CASE OF CAROL

Carol, a 39-year-old Caucasian female, entered counseling in the fall of 1993. Her presenting concern at the intake interview was that she desired to "know herself better" and that she wanted to learn more about her strengths and weaknesses in order to make a decision about her career direction. Carol's most recent employment experience involved her being fired due to a "conflict with the management." Carol reported that this experience "shot holes" in her self-esteem. She had been employed as a produce manager for a local health food store. Carol had been doing this type of work for the past 15 years. She reported a loss of interest in this occupation due to the work schedule (late nights and early mornings) and the low pay. She did report that she loved the task of putting together creative food displays. During the first session she also expressed an interest in becoming self-employed and doing woodworking.

Carol had taken approximately 2 years of coursework at a community college in California and, at the time she entered counseling, was enrolled in a course to be trained as an emergency medical technician. In addition, Carol was enrolled in a woodworking class at the local vocational-technical school. She talked about being interested in exploring a variety of occupational options. For instance, she stated that she had an interest in acquiring more information about physical therapy and carpentry. In exploring the former option, Carol stated that she had a strong dislike for studying science. Given the need to study science-related topics in a physical therapy curriculum, Carol decided to reconsider her interest in this occupation. Her current occupational interest seemed to be more related to her woodworking class. The instructor of this class had been very supportive of her and she felt as though she had developed some skills in this line of work. As a result, Carol had started doing carpentry projects for clients the instructor had referred to her.

Concerning her family background, Carol had two brothers and one sister. Carol was the only one in her family not living in California. She reported that her relationship with her father was strained. She felt that he was emotionally distant and highly critical of her. Her father was employed as a salesperson and her mother was a full-time homemaker. Until 1990, Carol had been living in a community that was focused on the study of Eastern religion. She left this community because she perceived the leader to be dishonest and abusive.

Carol's C-DAC Results

Adult Career Concerns Inventory

Number of Concerns Rated 4 (Considerable) or 5 (Great)

Exploration Stage
Crystallization 5
Specification 3
Implementation 5
Total 13

Establishment Stage
Stabilizing 2
Consolidating 4
Advancing 4
Total 10

Maintenance Stage
Holding 4
Updating 5
Innovating 4
Total 13

Disengagement Stage
Deceleration 0
Retirement Plan 2
Retirement Living 0
Total 2

(continued)

Occupational Stress Inventory

(Reported in T-Scores)

Occupational Roles Questionnaire:
Role Overload 40
Role Insufficiency 68
Role Ambiguity 60
Role Boundary 58
Responsibility 46
Physical Environment 45

Personal Strain Questionnaire:
Vocational Strain 49
Psychological Strain 52
Interpersonal Strain 50
Physical Strain 48

Personal Resources Questionnaire:
Recreation 55
Self-Care 51
Social Support 60
Rational/Cognitive Coping 52

Strong Interest Inventory

Academic Comfort 21
Introversion-Extroversion 60

Themes:
Realistic .... High 58
Artistic .... Average 51
Enterprising .... Mod. Low 35
Social .... Low 32
Conventional .... Low 31
Investigative .... Low 29

Basic Interests
High: Mechanical Activities 64
         Agriculture 61

Occupations:
Realistic:
Carpentry 57
Electrician 52
Vocational Agriculture Teacher 52
Emergency Medical Technician 51
Forester 47
Artistic:
Chef 49

(continued)

The Values Scale:

(Ratings Range from 1 = Low to 4 = High)

4.0	Autonomy
3.8	Ability Utilization
3.8	Social Relations
3.8	Creative
3.8	Personal Development
3.6	Achievement
3.6	Aesthetics
3.6	Economic Rewards
3.6	Life Style
3.6	Economic Security
3.4	Altruism
3.4	Physical Activity
3.2	Advancement
3.2	Working Conditions
3.0	Authority
3.0	Social Interaction
3.0	Cultural Identity
2.8	Variety
2.6	Prestige
1.8	Physical Prowess
1.4	Risk

The Salience Inventory

(Ratings Range from 1 = Low to 4 = High)

	Study	Work	Community Service	Home & Family	Leisure Activities
Participation	3.2	3.4	2.2	3.4	3.1
Commitment	4.0	3.6	2.4	3.9	3.6
Values Expectations	2.1	2.8	2.2	3.1	3.0

Using the C-DAC Battery with Carol

The results of the Occupational Roles Questionnaire of the Occupational Stress Inventory provided useful information concerning the stressors Carol was experiencing at the time she completed the assessment instruments. For instance, her score on the Role Insufficiency Scale (68) indicated that Carol was experiencing a poor fit between her skills and the job she was performing at the time she completed the assessment instruments. There also was the possibility that she was feeling as if her career was not progressing and that her needs for recognition and success were not being met.

An examination of her scores on the Personal Strain Questionnaire, however, suggests that Carol was not experiencing high levels of strain.

This was probably due to her effective use of coping resources as indicated by her scores on the Personal Resources Questionnaire.

Much of the counseling process with Carol was focused on self-exploration for the purpose of career decision making. That is, her interests, values, skills, and role involvements were examined in order to focus on a career direction. Carol reported a high interest in creative endeavors as well as "hands-on" activities. Woodworking was an emerging interest for her. She was enrolled in a woodworking class at the local vocational-technical school and found this to be a very enjoyable experience. She felt good about this type of work and identified an interest in carpentry with a tentative long-term goal of becoming more skilled at cabinet making.

The results of the ACCI suggested that Carol had considerable or great concern with tasks involving clarifying her ideas about the type of work she would really enjoy as well as identifying ways in which she could implement a choice once it was identified (Exploration stage concerns). Additional concerns related to improving her skills within a specific field (Maintenance stage concerns). These concerns are of interest because much of the counseling process involved exploring Carol's questions about whether to pursue work in the area of woodworking. More specifically, Carol wondered about being able to tolerate the male-dominated atmosphere in which much of her work would occur. She also was concerned about whether the goal of becoming a cabinet maker was economically viable. In essence, Carol had career concerns that focused on planning issues (e.g., How would I continue to develop my skills in carpentry? How would I go about starting my own business? How would I handle the sometimes "crude" behavior of males in the job?), and the need to acquire more information about her proposed occupation and the degree of fit between the occupation of carpentry and her interests, values, and skills (e.g., Is it possible to implement my goal and survive financially? Would cabinet making allow me to express my creativity? Would starting my own business provide me with the type of autonomy I desire?).

Her interest in woodworking was supported by the results of the SII. Carol had high scores on the Realistic theme and similar interests to those employed in the occupations of carpentry and electrician. Her preference in working with things rather than people was supported by her score on the Introversion-Extroversion Scale (60). Although Carol had noted an interest in exploring various educational options, she also stated that academic experiences needed to be tied into specified goals in order for her to persevere. That she tended to see education as a means to an end was supported by her Academic Comfort score of 21.

Carol's scores on the VS reinforced the kinds of needs, interests, and goals she had described in the counseling process. That is, the values of creativity, autonomy, ability utilization, personal development, and economic security were some of the values that Carol had identified as being important for her to consider in her career decision making. For instance, she stated that making an income that would provide her with the type of lifestyle she desired was important to her. Having time off during the day so that she could take classes related to her work and read in the area of spiritual development were specific lifestyle considerations Carol mentioned in counseling. That the idea of starting her own business was appealing to her was reflected in her VS score for autonomy. Carol also felt that woodworking offered her the opportunity for creative expression, especially in the area of cabinet making.

The SI provided Carol with the opportunity to examine the life roles in which she was participating. Scores on this assessment indicated that Carol spent much of her time participating in the roles of student, worker, home and family, and leisurite. It is interesting to note that her scores on the Commitment Scale were consistently higher than her scores on the Participation Scale, with the most dramatic difference in this regard being within the role of student. In exploring this difference, Carol noted that she would like to participate more in the student role, but felt that the lack of a career goal was holding her back. She thought that as her commitment to a career direction became stronger, she would be more involved in taking classes that were related to her career choice.

Another consistent pattern within Carol's scores on the SI was that her values expectations scores were relatively low. She did not expect to be able to express key values in the roles of student, worker, or community service. Although Carol's low score on the Values Expectation scale for community service is consistent with her scores on the Participation scale and the Commitment scale, her low scores in work and study may be more problematic. That is, if she is not hopeful that work will allow her to express important values, then it is possible that her commitment to the career decision-making process, as well as her participation in work, may suffer. The fact that Carol was fired from her last job and the effects of this incident on her self-esteem were issues that were explored early in the counseling relationship. It also was suggested to her that by identifying a career goal that was in tune with her values, skills, interests, and lifestyle needs, she may experience more opportunities for expressing her values in the future.

As counseling progressed, Carol became more confident about pursuing work as a carpenter. Through information interviewing she was able to find an accomplished carpenter who offered her employment and was willing to serve as a mentor for her. Carol terminated counseling with the career plan of pursuing the occupation of carpentry and accepting a position with her new found mentor.

THE CASE OF WILLIAM

William, a 38-year-old African American male with a college degree in criminal justice and biology (received in 1981), entered counseling in the spring of 1993. He sought career counseling as a way to explore his career options. At the time he entered counseling, William was employed as a surgical laboratory technician. Although he initially enjoyed this work, it had become boring and routine for him. He reported that the most enjoyable parts of this job were taking patient case histories and working with trauma cases. He noted that he was interested in pursuing an occupation that would provide him with more challenge and more opportunities for personal development. William described himself as "competitive," "creative," "verbally skilled," and a person who wanted "to make a difference."

William's work history reflected a variety of positions in different fields. For example, he had worked as a police officer, a salesperson for IBM, and as an advertising executive for several national companies. He obtained his current position after first serving as an emergency room volunteer and then being hired as a "lab tech," first in primary care and then in surgery. His current plans were to explore career options within the field of medical science.

William was first exposed to the field of medicine by his mother, who had been employed as a nurse. His father was a contractor who worked as a homebuilder and developer. William's family relationships were very important to him and he placed a great deal of importance on being able to spend time with his own children (ages 3 and 7) and his spouse.

William's C-DAC Results

Occupational Stress Inventory

(Reported in T-Scores)

Occupational Roles Questionnaire:
Role Overload 54
Role Insufficiency 74
Role Ambiguity 49
Role Boundary 68
Responsibility 64
Physical Environment 80

Personal Strain Questionnaire
Vocational Strain 53
Psychological Strain 44
Interpersonal Strain 48
Physical Strain 38

(continued)

Personal Resources Questionnaire
  Recreation 52
  Self-care 58
  Social Support 38
  Rational/Cognitive Coping 59

Strong Interest Inventory

  Academic Comfort: 68
  Introversion-Extroversion: 26

  Themes:
    Social .... Very High 74
    Conventional .... Very High 73
    Investigative .... Very High 68
    Enterprising .... High 62
    Realistic .... High 61
    Artistic .... Average 50

  Basic Interests:
    Very High: Medical Service 73
                Medical Science 71
                Military Activities 70
                Social Service 70
                Science 70
                Public Speaking 68
                Religious Activities 67
                Office Practice 67
                Law/Policies 65

    High: Nature 59
                Mechanical Activities 59
                Business Management 58
                Domestic 57
                Athletics 57

  Occupations:
    Nursing Home Administrator 65
    School Administrator 64
    Nurse, RN 63
    YWCA/YMCA Director 61
    Executive Housekeeper 61
    Dietician 60
    Public Administrator 58
    Minister 58
    Food Service Manager 57

(continued)

The Values Scale:

(Ratings Range from 1 = Low to 4 = High)

4.0 .... Ability Utilization
3.8 .... Altruism
3.8 .... Personal Development
3.6 .... Authority
3.6 .... Creativity
3.4 .... Achievement
3.4 .... Life Style
3.4 .... Advancement
3.0 .... Working Conditions
2.8 .... Aesthetics
2.8 .... Physical Activity
2.8 .... Economic Security
2.6 .... Social Interaction
2.6 .... Variety
2.6 .... Cultural Identity
2.4 .... Economic Rewards
2.2 .... Risk
2.0 .... Physical Prowess
1.4 .... Social Relations
1.2 .... Prestige

Adult Career Concerns Inventory

Number of concerns rated 4 (Considerable) or 5 (Great)

Exploration Stage
Crystallization 4
Specification 3
Implementation 2
Total 9

Establishment Stage
Stabilizing 0
Consolidating 2
Advancing 2
Total 4

Maintenance Stage
Holding 0
Updating 4
Innovating 4
Total 8

Disengagement Stage
Deceleration 0
Retirement Plan 0
Retirement Living 1
Total 1

(continued)

The Salience Inventory

(Ratings Range from 1 = Low to 4 = High)

	Study	Work	Community Service	Home & Family	Leisure Activities
Participation	4.0	4.0	3.9	4.0	2.6
Commitment	4.0	4.0	4.0	3.9	1.8
Values Expectations	3.8	3.8	3.9	3.8	2.1

Using the C-DAC Battery With William

The results of the Occupational Stress Inventory for William are noteworthy in that his Occupational Stress scores reflect high levels of the role insufficiency, role boundary, responsibility, and stressors in the physical environment. He reported a lack of challenge in his current occupation (surgical laboratory technician) and a high level of stress due to the hectic nature of the operating room atmosphere. Remarkably, William reported relatively little strain as a result of these stressors. The lack of strain is probably due to his strong coping skills, especially in the areas of self-care and rational/cognitive coping. William noted that he paid a great deal of attention to his diet and was careful to exercise on a regular basis. He stated that he had learned how to be a systematic problem solver from his parents and grandparents. As a result, he had a high level of self-efficacy when he was presented with a challenging situation.

William did, however, obtain a low score in the area of social support (T-score of 38). In discussing this score, William related that he had very few close friends and, therefore, experienced little social support outside of his immediate family. He also described himself as "very competitive." Ways were discussed in which his competitiveness could be helpful at some times and problematic in other situations. Concerning the latter, he felt that in order to compete he could not be open about his feelings of dissatisfaction and unsureness, especially as they related to his current and future career options. He felt that being open in these ways would be viewed by others as an indication of his "being weak" or "incompetent." Although he stated that he learned this from his father, it also was true that the low number of African Americans employed in occupations within medical science contributed to William's perceived need to present a confident and self-assured attitude. One result of these behaviors was that William was perceived by others as distant and aloof. The benefits to be gained by his being willing to share more honestly with others (e.g., friendship, less pressure on himself, time spent with family could be more enjoyable) were discussed. The counselor related that William had shared his confusion and questions with him and that he had very positive perceptions of him. William identified two people with whom he was willing to develop honest and more open friendships. He also identified how he could go about accomplishing this with them.

The results of the ACCI helped to put his career concerns into focus. He expressed a great amount of concern for the tasks of crystallization and specification (5.0). At the beginning of career counseling, William knew that he wanted more challenge in his work and more contact with people. He also felt it was important that he "make a difference" in life.

Rather than engaging in broad career exploration, however, William stated that he was interested in exploring occupational options within the field of medical service. This was reflected in the fact that he had expressed great concern (5.0) with the Maintenance stage tasks of updating and innovating. Given this rather focused career exploration, William initially decided to explore career options that were in the area of medical science—specifically, the occupations of dentist and physician. In order to get more information about his aptitude for these two occupations, he made plans for taking the Medical College Admission Test and the Dental Admission Test.

The scores of the SII indicated that William's interests were, for the most part, in line with the occupational options he was considering. That is, his academic comfort score (68) reflected his fondness for academic activities. He also had very high interest in the investigative theme and in the areas of medical service (73), medical science (71), and science (70).

It also was the case that William's profile on the SII was elevated. He had very high interest in social and conventional activities in addition to his very high interest in the investigative area. His lowest occupational theme score was in the artistic theme (50). It is likely that this elevation in scores was due to his diverse interests. In fact, his numerous jobs in different occupational fields (e.g., police work, advertising, medical service) reflected this diversity in interests.

A major issue in career counseling with William, therefore, was helping him understand the difficulty many people with elevated profiles have in making career decisions. That is, there is often a reluctance to commit to an occupation due to the perception that it limits opportunities for expressing a wide range of diverse interests. Because of this, William found it very useful to discuss his interests in light of the additional information provided in the results of the C-DAC battery (i.e., values and life role salience).

William's interests also were discussed in light of his decision to focus his career exploration on the occupations of dentistry and medicine. We explored ways in which he thought he would be able to express his interests in these two occupations. We also explored possible outlets that would provide William with opportunities to express his diverse interests.

For instance, he was very involved in his church (religious activities) and he spent time with his family participating in recreational activities (domestic and athletic interests). As the SII results were reviewed with William, he often referred to core values that seemed to be driving his decision to focus his career exploration on dentistry and medicine.

Scores from the VS were reviewed in order to provide a vehicle for further elaboration of William's most important values. His parents served as role models for him in this regard. William recounted how he would go with his mother (a nurse) when she would visit her patients (both at their homes and in the hospital). He also talked about how his father (a homebuilder) would routinely not collect money owed to him if he felt that a family was legitimately unable to pay. In essence, his parents were excellent models of values such as altruism and ability utilization. From watching his parents he stated that he learned that "life is about relationships." Any new career options would need to provide him with the opportunity to express the values and lessons he had learned from his parents.

As values were such a key ingredient for his decision making, William's values were examined in light of the two occupational options he had chosen to focus on (dentistry and medicine). Although both options provided him with opportunities to express his most important values (i.e., ability utilization, altruism, personal development, authority, autonomy, and creativity), William felt that medicine was the better choice for his skills and values. He had information about this occupation as a result of the early life exposure to medicine that he received from his mother and the experiences of his current job. Concerning the latter, he especially enjoyed the part of his job that involved taking case histories from patients (this job task provided him with opportunities to express his interests in the social theme). He reported that he thought that being a family practitioner would be an option that would allow him to "make a difference" and provide a service to patients with whom he would have ongoing relationships (examples of more social theme goals).

There were two major concerns William expressed relative to pursuing admission into medical school: (1) He was fearful that he would not be admitted, and (2) he was concerned that being a physician would require him to sacrifice his family life. William was very reluctant to discuss the first concern. This reluctance was related to his earlier comments about being "competitive" and the meaning he attached to being denied admission. He also decided that it would be helpful to spend more time conducting interviews with physicians who also were African Americans. The latter step proved to be very useful in providing him with more information about the nature of medical school in general. It also was useful in allowing William to conceptualize himself as a physician (who also was African American).

William's second concern related to the role conflict between being highly committed to work as well as to home and family. William's scores on the SI reinforced this conflict (4.0 for Commitment to Home and Family and Commitment to Work). He was uneasy about the prospect of sacrificing his time with his family. Once again, he felt that it would be helpful to him if he were able to talk to physicians about strategies they use in order to permit participation in home and family activities. He also planned to discuss this issue with his wife and children. By talking with them, he could get more information as to how they felt about the prospect of his being in an occupation that required a significant amount of time. He also could enlist their help in identifying creative ways to spend time together when the time demands of his job became extreme.

Reviewing the results of the C-DAC battery with William served as a vehicle for exploring many of the questions and insecurities he had concerning two occupational fields (i.e., dentistry and medicine). The assessment review process helped him to clarify his goals and make plans for dealing with potential areas of conflict that could arise in medical school and after he became a physician. The strategy of information interviewing provided him with more data relative to the training requirements and occupational demands inherent in the field of medicine. It also provided William with the opportunity to talk with other African Americans about their experiences in becoming (and being) physicians. Collectively, these experiences helped him to accomplish the tasks of specifying and implementing an occupational choice within the field of medicine. After preparing for, and taking, the Medical College Admission Test, William applied, was admitted, and decided to accept, an offer of admission to medical school.

SUMMARY

Using the C-DAC battery is an effective approach to helping adults examine and clarify their role self-concepts (Super, 1990). The assessments that comprise the battery provide important information relative to the issues of career concerns, values, and life role salience. The interpretation of the assessment results often provides adult career counseling clients with opportunities for examining the process by which they organize their career thoughts—what others refer to as the meaning-making process (Carlsen, 1988). Additionally, the incorporation of the Occupational Stress Inventory provides a holistic framework for identifying and coping with career issues.

Overall, the C-DAC battery is an excellent tool for fostering occupational self-concept clarification and implementation and the mastery of the career developmental tasks. As Super (1990) has noted, using the C-DAC model with adults enhances "the development of the counselee and of his or her career, so that he or she may find fulfillment in it" (p. 253).

Epilogue

Donald E. Super was a giant in the career development field for half a century. Most of his work can be summarized as involving trying to understand the many determinants of career development, tying all these together into a "segmental theory," and devising a career counseling approach that addresses these determinants while recognizing the interrelationship of personal and vocational development. His achievements were many, and he left us with still more work remaining to be done, including converging major career development theories and extending the application of the C-DAC model.

One of Super's wishes toward the end of his life was to convene all major career development theorists and arrive at an integrated view of the process (Super, 1994). He thought enough research and speculating about career development theory had been done to provide a basis for pulling together all that is known into a more holistic picture of the process so that no view stood alone, but only in relation to others.

Other directions for Super's work reflect his self-concept, the implementation of which demonstrated that one's age is not necessarily related to the career development stage he or she may be living. Super did not think of himself, until the last year of his life, as being in the Decline stage of his Life Stages and Substages model, generally characteristic of people from ages 60 to 70. He described himself, rather, as always "innovating" and as one who wanted to be on "the cutting edge" of his specialty, a developmental task of people typically aged 40 to 60 found in the Maintenance life stage.

Part of the way he accomplished this was through advancement of the Career Development, Assessment, and Counseling (C-DAC) model (Super et al. 1992) described in this book.

Super was interested in further studying this approach to understand how it could be more effectively used in career counseling. To that end, a research team consisting of the authors of this book was formed to conduct various studies. So far, research has been done on the relationship of Strong Interest Inventory "flat" profiles to career maturity, adults returning to the workplace have been profiled on the Adult Career Concerns Inventory, two studies on how personality preferences relate to career maturity have been conducted, and this book about the C-DAC model and how it can be used with high school students, college students, and adults has been completed. This team will continue to pursue Super's interest in understanding the applicability of the C-DAC approach, and intends to extend research focused on applications of the C-DAC model with high school students, undergraduate students, and adults.

Beyond this, Super was curious about how the C-DAC approach could be used with various groups, including Mexican Americans, African Americans, clients in other countries, and women. His earlier research, as part of the Career Pattern Study, was with a group of young men, and Super continued to be interested in how his model of career counseling could be extended to a wider variety of people.

The effort to achieve this has resulted in a number of convention and conference presentations at the state, regional, and national levels focused on the theoretical basis of the C-DAC approach and how to use it in case studies with clients representing gender and cultural differences. Research describing the career development characteristics of Mexican Americans has been done in Austin, Texas; a doctoral student at the University of North Carolina at Greensboro has completed a dissertation on the relationship of personality preferences to the career maturity of Mexican Americans and Anglo Americans; and other research on the career development of women and African Americans is under way and will continue.

These are notable attempts at extending Super's ideas to a broader range of people. It also is important, however, to pursue his interest to understand the usefulness of career development theory and traditional career counseling procedures for other countries.

At the time of Super's death, an international consortium of 14 nations called the Work Importance Study was exploring applications of the C-DAC model to other cultures. The initial work of this consortium resulted in The Values Scale and The Salience Inventory. This effort should proceed to explore the appropriateness of career development theory for other populations, devise ways to provide effective career counseling for persons of varied backgrounds, and modify the C-DAC instruments for the widest possible use.

There is at least one more wish that Donald Super would have had for the future of the career development field. This involves the further popularization of study and professional practice in this aspect of our profession, and the nurturing of young professionals to carry on this endeavor. He was fond of saying that he had more colleagues collaborating with him during the last 15 years of his life than he ever had before, and his hope was that he could continue to excite others to join him in his work (Osborne, 1996).

There is still much left to do. Part of it involves extending Super's half-century of career development research and practice in new ways and with other populations. It also involves disseminating these ideas and applied procedures to a wider audience, and involving other professionals in joining the effort to further develop the C-DAC approach.

This is the exciting promise of Donald E. Super's work and life. No greater tribute exists than the commitment of those who knew him to ensure that this promise is met.

References

Anastasi, A. (1988). *Psychological testing.* New York: Macmillan.

Anderson, W. P., & Niles, S. G. (1995). Career and personal concerns expressed by career counseling clients. *Career Development Quarterly, 43,* 240–245.

Arthur, M. B., Hall, D. T., & Lawrence, B. (Eds.). (1989). *Handbook of career theory.* New York: Cambridge University Press.

Bandura, A. (1977). *Social learning theory.* Englewood Cliffs, NJ: Prentice-Hall.

Bartley, D. L. (1989). *The effect of training in vocational education on the work values of selected criminal offenders in Texas' mentally retarded offender program.* Unpublished doctoral dissertation, Texas A & M University, College Station.

Bloom, B. S. (1964). *Stability and change in human characteristics.* New York: Wiley.

Borow, H. (1982). Career development theory and instrumental outcomes of career education: A critique. In J. D. Krumboltz and D. A. Hames (eds.), *Assessing career development.* Mountain View, CA: Mayfield.

Brown, D., Brooks, L., & Associates. (1990). *Career choice and development.* San Francisco: Jossey-Bass.

Brown, S. D., & Lent, R. W. (1984). *Handbook of counseling psychology.* New York: John Wiley & Sons.

Buehler, C. (1933). *Der menschliche lebenslauf als psychologisches problem.* [The human life-course as a subject for psychological study]. Leipsig: Hirzel.

Campbell, D. P., Borgen, S., Eastes, C. B., Johannson, C. B., & Peterson, R. A. (1968). A set of Basic Interest Scales for the Strong Vocational Interest Blank for men. *Journal of Applied Psychology Monographs, 52,* no. 6, part 2.

Campbell, D. P., & Fiske, D. W. (1959). Convergent and discriminant validation by the multitrait-multimethod matrix. *Psychological Bulletin, 56,* 81–105.

Campbell, D. P., & Hansen, J. C. (1972). A merger in vocational interest research: Applying Holland's theory to Strong's data. *Journal of Vocational Behavior, 2,* 353–376.

Carlsen, M. B. (1988). *Meaning-making: Therapeutic processes in adult development.* New York: W. W. Norton.

Cochran, L. (1992). The career project. *Journal of Career Development, 18,* 187–198.

Crites, J. O. (1969). *Vocational psychology.* New York: McGraw-Hill.

Crites, J. O. (1973). *Theory and research handbook for the Career Maturity Inventory.* Monterey, CA: CTB/McGraw-Hill.

Crites, J. O. (1974). A review of major approaches. *The Counseling Psychologist, 4* (3), 12–17.

Crites, J. O. (1978). Career Maturity Inventory. Monterey, CA: CTB/McGraw-Hill.

Cron, W. L., & Slocum, J.W. (1986). The influence of career stages on salespeoples' job attitudes, work perception, and performance. *Journal of Marketing Research, 23,* 119–129.

Davidson, P. E., & Anderson, H. D. (1937). *Occupational mobility in an American community.* Stanford, CA: Stanford University Press.

DISCOVER: A computer-based career development and counselor support system. (1984). Iowa City, IA: American College Testing Foundation.

Dupont, P. (1992). Concurrent and predictive validity of the Career Development Inventory. *International Journal for the Advancement of Counselling, 15,* 163–173.

Dykeman, B. F. (1983). Correlation of vocational maturity and components of vocational maturity with rated work effectiveness. *Education, 104* (1), 80–84.

Farr, M. J. (1993). *The complete guide for occupational exploration.* Indianapolis, IN: JIST Works.

Fisher, I. (1989). *Midlife change.* Unpublished doctoral dissertation, Teachers College, Columbia University, New York.

Flanagan, J. C. (1973). Some pertinent findings of project talent. *Vocational Guidance Quarterly, 22,* 92–96.

Fouad, N. A. (1992). Comments on Super's theory and C-DAC model. *Journal of Counseling & Development, 71* (1), 81–82.

Gelso, C. J., & Fretz, B. R. (1992). *Counseling psychology.* Orlando, FL: Harcourt Brace Jovanovich.

Ginzberg, E. (1971). *Career guidance.* New York: McGraw-Hill.

Goldman, L. (1971). *Using tests in counseling* (2nd ed.). Englewood Cliffs, NJ: Prentice-Hall.

Gribbons, W. D., & Lohnes, P. R. (1968). *Emerging careers.* New York: Teachers College Press.

Gribbons, W. D., & Lohnes, P. R. (1982). *Careers in theory and experience: A twenty-year longitudinal study.* Albany, NY: State University of New York Press.

Halpin, G., Ralph, J., & Halpin, G. (1990). The Adult Career Concerns Inventory: Validity and reliability. *Measurement and Evaluation in Counseling and Development, 22,* 196–202.

Hansen, J. C. (1985). *Users guide to the SVIB-SCII.* Palo Alto, CA: Consulting Psychologists Press.

Hansen, J. C. (1994). The Strong Interest Inventory—Revised. Palo Alto, CA: Consulting Psychologists Press.

Hansen, J. C., & Campbell, D. P. (1985). *Manual of the SVIB-SCII.* Palo Alto, CA: Consulting Psychologists Press.

Hansen, J. C., & Johansson, R. W. (1972). The application of Holland's vocational model to the Strong Vocational Interest Blank for Women. *Journal of Vocational Behavior, 2,* 479–493.

Harmon, L. W., Hansen, J. C., Borgen, F. H., & Hammer, A. L. (1994). *Strong Interest Inventory applications and technical guide.* Palo Alto, CA: Consulting Psychologists Press.

Harrington, T. F., & O'Shea, A. J. (1992). *Manual for the Harrington-O'Shea Career Decision-Making—Revised.* Circle Pines, MN: American Guidance Service.

Healy, C. C. (1990). Reforming career appraisals to meet the needs of clients in the 1990s. *The Counseling Psychologist, 18,* 214–226.

Helms, F. L. (1991). *An investigation of the relationship between age, commitment to work, commitment to study, commitment to home, and career maturity among traditional and nontraditional college students.* Unpublished doctoral dissertation, Auburn University, Montgomery, Alabama.

Herr, E. L., & Cramer, S. H. (1992). *Career guidance and counseling through the life span: Systematic approaches.* (p. 378). New York: HarperCollins, p. 378.

Holland, J. L. (1959). A theory of vocational choice. *Journal of Counseling Psychology, 6,* 35–45.

Holland, J. L. (1973). *Making vocational choices: A theory of careers.* Lutz, FL: Psychological Assessment Resources.

Holland, J. L. (1974). Vocational guidance for everyone. *Educational Research, 3,* 9–15.

Holland, J. L. (1985). *Making vocational choices: A theory of vocational personalities and work environments* (2nd ed.). Englewood Cliffs, NJ: Prentice-Hall.

Isaacson, L. E. (1985). *Basics of career counseling.* Boston, MA: Allyn & Bacon.

Isaacson, L. E., & Brown, D. (1993). *Career information, career counseling, & career development* (5th ed.). Boston, MA: Allyn & Bacon.

Johnson, S. D. (1985). Career Development Inventory. *Test Critiques, 4,* 132–143.

Jordaan, J. P., & Heyde, M. B. (1979). *Vocational maturity during the high school years.* New York: Teachers College Press.

Kleinberg, J. L. (1976). Adolescent correlates of occupational stability and change. *Journal of Vocational Behavior, 9,* 219–232.

Krau, E. (1989). The transition in life domain salience and the modification of work values between high school and adult employment. *Journal of Vocational Behavior, 34,* 100–116.

Krumboltz, J. D. (1988). Career Beliefs Inventory. Palo Alto, CA: Consulting Psychologists Press.

Lokan, J. J. (1983). The factor structure of life and work values held by students in diverse cultures. In D. E. Super (Chairman), *Values and roles in diverse modern societies.* Symposium conducted at the meeting of the American Educational Research Association, Montreal, Canada.

Luzzo, D. A. (1993). A multi-trait, multi-method analysis of three career development measures. *Career Development Quarterly, 41* (4), 367–374.

Maccoby, M. (1981). *The leader: A new face for American management.* New York: Simon & Schuster.

Mahoney, D.J. (1986). *An exploration of the construct validity of a measure of adult vocational maturity.* Unpublished doctoral dissertation, Teachers College, Columbia University, New York.

McDaniels, C. (1989). *The changing workplace.* San Francisco: Jossey-Bass.

Miller, D. C., & Form, W. H. (1951). *Industrial sociology.* New York: Harper & Row.

Mitchell, L. K., & Krumboltz, J. D. (1990). Social learning approach to career decision making: Krumboltz's theory. In D. Brown, L. Brooks, & Associates, *Career choice and development* (pp. 145–196). San Francisco: Jossey-Bass.

Montross, D. H., & Shinkman, C. J. (1992). *Career development: Theory and practice* (2nd ed.). Springfield, IL: Charles C Thomas.

Morrison, R. F. (1977). Career adaptivity: The effective adaptation of managers to changing role demands. *Journal of Applied Psychology, 62,* 549–558.

Murphy, P., & Burck, H. (1976). Career development of men at mid-life. *Journal of Vocational Behavior, 9,* 337–342.

Myers, I. B. (1993). *Introduction to type.* Palo Alto, CA: Consulting Psychologists Press.

Myers, R. A., Lindeman, R. H., Forrest, D. J., & Super, D. E. (1971). *Preliminary report: Assessment of the first year of the Educational and Career Exploration System.* New York: Teachers College, Columbia University.

Nevill, D. D., & Super, D. E. (1984). Work role salience as a determinant of career maturity in high school students. *Journal of Vocational Behavior, 25* (1), 30–44.

Nevill, D. D., & Super D. E. (1986a). *Manual for The Salience Inventory.* Palo Alto, CA: Consulting Psychologists Press.

Nevill, D. D., & Super, D. E. (1986b). *Manual for The Salience Inventory: Theory, application, and research.* Palo Alto, CA: Consulting Psychologists Press.

Nevill, D. D., & Super, D. E. (1986c). The Salience Inventory. Palo Alto, CA: Consulting Psychologists Press.

Nevill, D. D., & Super, D. E. (1986d). *The Values Scale theory, application, and research.* Palo Alto, CA: Consulting Psychologists Press.

Nevill, D. D., & Super, D. E. (1988). Career maturity and commitment to work in university students. *Journal of Vocational Behavior, 32* (2), 139–151.

Nevill, D. D., & Super, D. E. (1989a). The Values Scale. Palo Alto, CA: Consulting Psychologists Press.

Nevill, D. D., & Super, D. E. (1989b). *The Values Scale: Theory, application, and research.* Palo Alto, CA: Consulting Psychologists Press.

Niles, S. G., Sowa, C. J., & Laden, J. (1994). Life role participation and commitment as predictors of college student development. *Journal of College Student Development, 35,* 159–163.

Niles, S. G., & Usher, C. H. (1993). Applying the Career Development Assessment and Counseling model to the case of Rosie. *The Career Development Quarterly, 42,* 61–66.

Ogbu, J. U. (1990). Cultural model, identity, and literacy. In J. Stigler, R. Shweder, & G. Herdt (Eds.), *Cultural psychology: Essays on comparative human development* (pp. 520–541). Cambridge: Cambridge University Press.

Osborne, W. L. (1996). Donald E. Super: Yesterday and tomorrow. In G. Walz & R. Feller (Eds.), *Career transitions in turbulent times: Exploring work, learning and careers,* (pp. 67–75). Greensboro, NC: ERIC/CASS.

Osborne, W. L., & Usher, C. H. (1994). A Super approach: Training career educators, career counselors and researchers. *Journal of Career Development, 20* (3), 219–225.

Osipow, S. (1990). Convergence in theories of career choice and development: Review and prospect. *Journal of Vocational Behavior, 36,* 122–131.

Osipow, S. H., & Spokane, A. R. (1987). *Manual for the Occupational Stress Inventory.* Odessa, FL: Psychological Assessment Resources.

Parsons, F. (1909). *Choosing a vocation.* Boston: Houghton Mifflin.

Pope, J. (1989). *Voluntary career change among executive women in mid-life.* Unpublished doctoral dissertation, University of Pittsburgh, Pittsburgh, Pennsylvania.

Prediger, D. J. (1974). The role of assessment in career guidance: A reappraisal. *Impact, 3,* 15–21.

Pryor, R. G. L. (1981). *Manual for the Work Aspect Preference Scale.* New South Wales: Department of Industrial Relations.

Raskin, P. M. (1987). *Vocational counseling: A guide for the practitioner.* New York: Teachers College Press.

Rogers, C. R. (1951). *Client-centered therapy.* Boston: Houghton Mifflin.

Savickas, M. L. (1993). Career counseling in the postmodern era. *Journal of Cognitive Psychotherapy: An International Quarterly, 7,* 205–215.

Savickas, M. L., Silling, S. M., & Schwartz, S. (1984). Time perspective in vocational maturity and career decision making. *Journal of Vocational Behavior, 25* (3), 258–269.

Seifert, K. H. (1991). Measures of career development and career choice behaviour. *Applied Psychology: An International Review, 40* (3), 245–267.

Shears, M. J. (1982, August). The construct validity of the WIS measures in Australia. In D. E. Super (Chairman), *The relative importance of work, reports from eight countries.* Symposium conducted at the meeting of the International Congress of Applied Psychology, Edinburgh.

SIGI PLUS: Counselor's manual. (1985). Princeton, NJ: Educational Testing Service.

Spokane, A. R. (1991). *Career intervention.* Englewood Cliffs, NJ: Prentice-Hall.

Stout, S. K., Slocum, J. W., & Cron, W. L. (1987). *Dynamics of the career plateauing process.* Working paper 87-073, E. L. Cox School of Business, Southern Methodist University, Dallas, Texas.

Strong, E. K., Jr. (1927). Vocational Interest Blank. Stanford, CA: Stanford University Press.

Strong, E. K., Jr. (1935). Predictive value of the Vocational Interest Test. *Journal of Educational Psychology, 26,* 332.

Strong, E. K., Jr. (1943). *Vocational interests of men and women.* Stanford, CA: Stanford University Press.

Strong, E. K., Campbell, D. P., & Hansen, J. C. (1985). Strong Interest Inventory. Palo Alto, CA: Consulting Psychologists Press.

Super, D. E. (1942). *The dynamics of vocational adjustment.* New York: Harper & Row.

Super, D. E. (1951). Vocational adjustment: Implementing a self-concept. *Occupations, 30,* 88–92.

Super, D. E. (1953). A theory of vocational development. *American Psychologist, 8,* 185–190.

Super, D. E. (1954). Career patterns as a basis for vocational counseling. *Journal of Counseling Psychology, 1,* 12–20.

Super, D. E. (1955). The dimensions and measurement of vocational maturity. *Teachers College Record, 57,* 151–163.

Super, D. E. (1957). *The psychology of careers.* New York: Harper & Row.

Super, D. E. (1969). Vocational development theory. *Counseling Psychologist, 1,* 2–30.

Super, D. E. (1970). The Work Values Inventory. Chicago: Riverside.

Super, D. E. (1973). The Work Values Inventory. In D. G. Zytowski (Ed.), *Contemporary approaches to interest measurement* (pp. 189–205). Minneapolis: University of Minnesota Press.

Super, D. E. (Ed.) (1974). *Measuring vocational maturity for counseling and evaluation.* Washington, D.C.: American Personnel and Guidance Association.

Super, D.E. (1977). Vocational maturity in midcareer. *Vocational Guidance Quarterly, 25,* 294–302.

Super, D.E. (1980). A life span, life space approach to career development. *Journal of Vocational Behavior, 16,* 282–298.

Super, D. E. (1983). Assessment in career guidance: Toward truly developmental counseling. *The Personnel and Guidance Journal, 61,* 555–562.

Super, D. E. (1984). Perspectives on the meaning and value of work. In N. Gysbers and Associates (Eds.). *Designing careers* (pp. 27–53). San Francisco: Jossey-Bass.

Super, D. E. (1985). Coming of age in Middletown: Careers in the making. *American Psychologist, 40,* 405–414.

Super, D. E. (1990). A life-span, life-space approach to career development. In D. Brown & L. Brooks & Associates. *Career choice and development* (pp. 167–261). San Francisco: Jossey-Bass.

Super, D. E. (1992). Response: The comments, the theory, and the model. *Journal of Counseling and Development, 71* (1), 83.

Super, D. E. (1994). A life span, life space perspective on convergence. In M. L. Savickas & R. W. Lent (Eds.). *Convergence in career development theories.* Palo Alto, CA: Consulting Psychologists Press.

Super, D. E., & Bachrach, P. (1957). *Scientific careers and vocational development theory.* New York: Teachers College Press.

Super, D. E., Kowalski, R. S., & Gotkin, E. H. (1967). *Floundering and trial after high school.* New York: Teachers College, Columbia University.

Super, D.E., & Kidd, J. M. (1979). Vocational maturity in adulthood: Toward turning a model into a measure. *Journal of Vocational Behavior, 14,* 255–270.

Super, D.E., & Knasel, F.G. (1981). Career development in adulthood: Some theoretical problems and a possible solution. *British Journal of Guidance and Counseling, 9,* 199–201.

Super, D. E., Osborne, W. L., Walsh, D. J., Brown, S. D., & Niles, S. G. (1992). Developmental career assessment and counseling: The C-DAC model. *Journal of Counseling and Development, 71,* 74–83.

Super, D. E., & Overstreet, P. L. (1960). *The vocational maturity of ninth-grade boys.* New York: Teachers College Press.

Super, D. E., Starishevsky, R., Matlin, N., & Jordaan, J. P. (1963). *Career development: Self-concept theory.* New York: College Entrance Examination Board.

Super, D. E., Thompson, A. S., Lindeman, R. H., Jordaan, J. P., & Myers, R. A. (1979). Career Development Inventory—School Form. Palo Alto, CA: Consulting Psychologists Press.

Super, D. E., Thompson, A. S., Lindeman, R. H., Jordaan, J. P., & Myers, R. A. (1988a). Adult Career Concerns Inventory. Palo Alto, CA: Consulting Psychologists Press.

Super, D. E., Thompson, A. S., Lindeman, R. H., Jordaan, J. P., & Myers, R. A. (1988b). Career Development Inventory. Palo Alto, CA: Consulting Psychologists Press.

Super, D. E., Thompson, A. S., Lindeman, R. H., Jordaan, J. P., & Myers, R. A. (1988c). *Career Development Inventory. Vol. 1. User's Manual.* Palo Alto, CA: Consulting Psychologists Press.

Sverko, B. (1982, August). The structure of work values: A national comparison. In D. E. Super (Chairman), *The relative importance of work, reports from eight countries.* Symposium conducted at the meeting of the International Association of Applied Psychology, Edinburgh.

Taylor, K. F. (1975). *Orientations to work.* Unpublished doctoral dissertation, University of Melbourne, Melbourne, Australia.

Torres, B. M. (1991). *The relationship between work values and job satisfaction of potential minority leaders in community colleges and technical institutes.* Unpublished doctoral dissertation, Texas A & M University, College Station, Texas.

U. S. Bureau of the Census (1993). *Statistical abstract of the United States: 1993* (113th ed.). Washington, D.C.: U.S. Government Printing Office.

U.S. Department of Labor, Bureau of Labor Statistics. (1991). *Dictionary of occupational titles* (4th Ed.). Washington, DC: U.S. Government Printing Office.

U.S. Department of Labor, Bureau of Labor Statistics. (1996). *Occupational outlook handbook, 1996–97 edition.* Washington, DC: U.S. Government Printing Office.

Usher, C. H., Carns, A. W., Carns, M. R., Jones, L., Wright, J., Garcia, J. L., & Wooten, H. R. (1994). Highlights of a career assessment project with ninth grade students: A collaborative effort between university and public school personnel. *TCA Journal, 22,* 29–34.

Varca, P. E., & Shaffer, G. S. (1982). Holland's theory: Stability of avocational interests. *Journal of Vocational Behavior, 21,* 288–298.

Veeder, S. P. (1991). *A descriptive comparison of nontraditional career women who are forming the entry life structure and nontraditional women who are completing the age thirty transition.* Unpublished doctoral dissertation, University of Pittsburgh, Pittsburgh, Pennsylvania.

Vocational Biographies. (1994). Sauk Centre, MN: Vocational Biographies, Inc.

Weinrach, S. G. (1979). Trait and factor counseling: Yesterday and today. In S. G. Weinrach (Ed.), *Career counseling: Theoretical and practical perspectives,* (pp. 59–69). New York: McGraw-Hill.

Weissberg, M., Berentsen, M., Cote, A., Cravey, B., & Heath, K. (1982). An assessment of the personal, career and academic needs of undergraduate students. *Journal of College Student Personnel, 23* (2), 115–122.

Westbrook, B. W., Sanford, E. E., & Donnelly, M. H. (1990). The relationship between career maturity test scores and appropriateness of career choices: A replication. *Journal of Vocational Behavior, 36,* 20–32.

Williamson, E. G. (1950). *Counseling adolescents.* New York: McGraw-Hill.

Wooten, H. R., & Hinkle, J. S. (1994). Career life planning with college student-athletes. *TCA Journal, 22,* 35–39.

Yates, L. V. (1990a). A note about values assessment of occupational and career stage age groups. *Measurement and Evaluation in Counseling and Development, 23* (1), 39–43.

Yates, L. (1990b). *The Values Scale: Assessment of adults involved in career development.* Unpublished manuscript.

Yost, E. B., & Corbishley, M. A. (1987). *Career counseling.* San Francisco: Jossey-Bass.

Zelkowitz, R. S. (1974). *The construction and validation of a measure of vocational maturity for adults.* Unpublished doctoral dissertation, Columbia University. Ann Arbor: University Microfilm 75-18, 456.

Zunker, V. G. (1990). *Using assessment results for career development* (3rd ed.). Pacific Grove, CA: Brooks/Cole.

Zytowski, D. (1988). Review of The Salience Inventory. In J. Kapes & M. Mastie (Eds.), *A counselor's guide to career assessment instruments* (2nd ed., pp.150–154). Alexandria, VA: National Career Development Association.

SUBJECT INDEX

A

Ability, identification of, 86

Academic Comfort Scale, in Strong Interest Inventory, 25

ACCI. *See* Adult Career Concerns Inventory (ACCI)

Adaptability
  in adulthood, 114
  definition of, 3
  factors in, 14

Adolescent career counseling. *See also under name, e.g., Carlos*
  developmental model of, 51–53
    versus classic matching model in, 51–52, 52t
  in ninth-grade students
    Laura, age 17, 65–69
    Joan, age 15, 59–65
    Carlos, age 14, 62–65
  theoretical basis of, 45–51

Adult Career Concerns Inventory (ACCI), 14–21
  administration and scoring of, 15–16
  in adolescents, 45
  in adult exploration of career options, 144, 146
  in adults, 42, 121–122
    average scores, 121t
    C-DAC sequence and, 129
    T-scores, 122f
  in C-DAC, 7
  in change of career direction, 137, 140
  definition of, 1
  planfulness assessment in, 14

for reentry career choice, 16, 17f
reliability of, 15
in sequence A, 41
in sequence B, 41
tasks in, 114–115
underlying factors in, 3
in unemployed architect, 133–134
use of, 13
validity of, 15

Adulthood. *See also* Personal and Career Development Center (PCDC)
  adaptability in, 114
  Adult Career Concerns Inventory in, 42, 115, 118, 120, 121–122
  career beliefs in, 127
  case studies in. *See also under name, e.g., Donald*
    career options, William, 142–148
    change in career direction, Carol, 136–141
    unemployed architect, Donald, 130–136
  C-DAC model in, 120, 129-130
    results for PCDC clients, 120–128
  comparison with adolescence, 113–114
  determinants in, 115–116
  leisure in, 128
  Life roles and, 117
  Occupational Stress Inventory in, 122–123, 123t, 124f
  readiness in. *See* Adaptability

AUTHOR INDEX